The Modern Husband by Henry Fielding

Henry Fielding was born at Sharpham Park, near Glastonbury, in Somerset on April 22nd 1707. His early years were spent on his parents' farm in Dorset before being educated at Eton.

An early romance ended disastrously and with it his removal to London and the beginnings of a glittering literary career; he published his first play, at age 21, in 1728.

He was prolific, sometimes writing six plays a year, but he did like to poke fun at the authorities. His plays were thought to be the final straw for the authorities in their attempts to bring in a new law. In 1737 The Theatrical Licensing Act was passed. At a stroke political satire was almost impossible. Fielding was rendered mute. Any playwright who was viewed with suspicion by the Government now found an audience difficult to find and therefore Theatre owners now toed the Government line.

Fielding was practical with the circumstances and ironically stopped writing to once again take up his career in the practice of law and became a barrister after studying at Middle Temple. By this time he had married Charlotte Craddock, his first wife, and they would go on to have five children. Charlotte died in 1744 but was immortalised as the heroine in both Tom Jones and Amelia.

Fielding was put out by the success of Samuel Richardson's Pamela, or Virtue Rewarded. His reaction was to spur him into writing a novel. In 1741 his first novel was published; the successful Shamela, an anonymous parody of Richardson's novel.

Undoubtedly the masterpiece of Fielding's career was the novel Tom Jones, published in 1749. It is a wonderfully and carefully constructed picaresque novel following the convoluted and hilarious tale of how a foundling came into a fortune.

Fielding was a consistent anti-Jacobite and a keen supporter of the Church of England. This led to him now being richly rewarded with the position of London's Chief Magistrate. Fielding continued to write and his career both literary and professional continued to climb.

In 1749 he joined with his younger half-brother John, to help found what was the nascent forerunner to a London police force, the Bow Street Runners. Fielding's ardent commitment to the cause of justice in the 1750s unfortunately coincided with a rapid deterioration in his health. Such was his decline that in the summer of 1754 he travelled, with Mary and his daughter, to Portugal in search of a cure. Gout, asthma, dropsy and other afflictions forced him to use crutches. His health continued to fail alarmingly.

Henry Fielding died in Lisbon two months later on October 8th, 1754.

ACT I
SCENE I
SCENE II
SCENE III
SCENE IV
SCENE V
SCENE VI
SCENE VII

Hæc ego non credam Venusinâ digna Lucernâ?
Hæc ego non agitem?
Cùm Leno accipiat Moechi bona, si capiendi
Jus nullum Uxori, doctus spectare Lacunar,
Doctus & ad Calicem vigilanti stertere Naso.
Juv. Sat. 1.

To the Right Honourable Sir Robert Walpole, Knight of the Most Noble Order of the Garter.

SIR,

While the Peace of Europe, and the Lives and Fortunes of so great a Part of Mankind, depend on Your Counsels, it may be thought an Offence against the publick Good to divert, by Trifles of this Nature, any of those Moments, which are so sacred to the Welfare of our Country.

But however ridicul'd or exploded the Muses may be, in an Age when their greatest Favourites are liable to the Censure and Correction of every Boy or Idiot, who shall have it in his power to satisfy the Wantonness of an evil Heart, at the Expence of the Reputation and Interest of the best Poet, yet has this Science been esteemed, honoured, protected, and often professed by the greatest Persons of Antiquity. Nations and the Muses have generally enjoyed the same Protectors.

The Reason of this is obvious: As the best Poets have owed their Reward to the greatest Heroes and Statesmen of their Times, so those Heroes have owed to the Poet that Posthumous Reputation, which is generally the only Reward that attends the greatest Actions. By them the Great and Good blaze out to Posterity, and triumph over the little Malice and Envy which once pursued them.

Protect therefore, Sir, an Art from which You may promise Your self such notable Advantages; when the little Artifices of Your Enemies, which You have surmounted, shall be forgotten, when Envy shall cease to misrepresent Your Actions, and Ignorance to misapprehend them. The Muses shall remember their Protector, and the wise Statesman the generous Patron, the stedfast Friend, and the true Patriot; but above all that Humanity and Sweetness of Temper, which shine thro' all your Actions, shall render the Name of Sir Robert Walpole dear to his no longer ungrateful Country.
That Success may attend all Your Counsels; that You may continue to preserve us from our Enemies Abroad, and to triumph over Your Enemies at Home, is the sincere Wish of,

SIR, Your most obliged, Most obedient humble Servant, Henry Fielding.

PROLOGUE

Spoken by Mr. WILKS

In early Youth, our Author first begun,
To Combat with the Follies of the Town;
Her want of Art, his unskill'd Muse bewail'd,
And where his Fancy pleas'd, his Judgment fail'd.
Hence, your nice Tastes he strove to entertain,
With unshap'd Monsters of a wanton Brain!
He taught Tom Thumb strange Victories to boast,
Slew Heaps of Giants, and thenkill'd a Ghost!
To Rules, or Reason, scorn'd the dull Pretence,
And fought your Champion, 'gainst the Cause of Sense!
At length, repenting Frolick Flights of Youth,
Once more he flies to Nature, and to Truth:
In Virtue's just Defence, aspires to Fame,
And courts Applause without the Applauder's Shame!
Impartial let your Praise, or Censure flow,
For, as he brings no Friend, he hopes to find no Foe.
His Muse in Schools too unpolite was bred,
To apprehend each Critick that can Read:
For, sure, no Man's Capacity's loss ample
Because he's been at Oxford or the Temple!
He shews but little Judgment, or discerning,
Who thinks Taste banish'd from the Seats of Learning.
Nor is less false, or scandalous th' Aspersion,
That such will ever damn their own Diversion.
But, Poets damn'd, like Thieves convicted, act,
Rail at their Jury, and deny the Fact!
To Night (yet Strangers to the Scene) you'll view,
A Pair of Monsters most entirely new!
Two Characters scarce ever found in Life.
A willing Cuckoldsells his willing Wife!
But, from whatever Clime the Creatures come,
Condemn 'em notbecause not found at home:
If then, true Nature in his Scenes you trace,
Not Scenes, that Comedy to Farce debase;
If Modern Vice detestable be shewn,
And vicious, as it is, he draws the Town;
Tho' no loud Laugh applaud the serious Page,
Restore the sinking Honour of the Stage!
The Stage which was not for low Farce design'd,
But to divert, instruct, and mend Mankind.

EPILOGUE

Spoken by Mrs. HERON

As Malefactors, on their dying Day,

Have always something, at the Tree, to say;
So I, before to Exile I go down,
With my hard hapless Fate would warn the Town.
Fatal Quadrille! Fly! Fly the tempting Evil!
For when our last Stake's lost, 'tis sure the Devil!
With curst Quadrille avoid my fatal Shame,
Or if you can'tat leastplay all the Game
Of spotless Fame, be chary as your Lives!
Keep wide of Proof, and you're the best of Wives!
Husbands most Faults, not publick made, connive at;
The Trip's a Triflewhen the Frailty's private.
What can a Poet hope, then, that reveals 'em?
The Fair might like the Play, whose Plot conceals 'em;
For who would favour Plays to be thus us'd,
None ever were by Operas abus'd!
Or could they warble Scandal out at random,
Where were the Harm, while none could understand 'em?
But I no more must hear those melting Strains
Condemn'd, alas! to Woods and lonely Plains!
Gay Masquerades, now, turn'd to Country–Fairs,
And croaking Rooks supply soft Eunuch Airs.
No Ring, no Mallno Rat, tat, tat, at Doors;
And, O hard Fate! for dear Quadrille All–Fours.
No more new Plays! but that's a small Offence,
Your Taste will shortly banish them from hence.
Yet ere I part, methinks, it were to wrong you,
Not to bequeath some Legacies among you.
My Reputation, I for Prudes intend,
In hopes their Strictness what's amiss will mend.
My young Gallants, let ancient Maidens kill,
And take my Husbandany Soul that will!
Our Author to the spotless Fair I give,
For his chaste Wife to grant him a Reprieve:
Whatever Faults to me may be imputed,
In her you view your Virtues unpolluted.
In her sweet Mind, even Age and wandring Youth
Must own the Transports of Connubial Truth:
Thus each Extreme is for Instruction meant,
And ever was the Stage's true Intent,
To give Reward to Virtue, Vice its Punishment.

Dramatis Personæ
MEN
LORD RICHLY
MR BELLAMANT
CAPT BELLAMANT
MR GAYWIT
MR MODERN
LORD LAZY

COLONEL COURTLY
MR WOODALL
CAPT MERIT
CAPT BRAVEMORE
SERVANT

WOMEN
LADY CHARLOTTE GAYWIT
MRS BELLAMANT
MRS MODERN
EMILIA
LATELY

SCENE LONDON.

ACT I

SCENE I

SCENE, Mrs. Modern's House.

Mrs. Modern at her Toilet: Lately attending.

MRS MODERN - Lud! this Creature is longer in sticking a Pin, than some People are in dressing a Head. Will you never have done fumbling?

LATELY - There, Maam, your Ladyship is drest.

MRS MODERN - Drest! ay, most frightfully drest, I am sure If it were not too late, I wou'd begin it all again. This Gown is wretchedly made, and does not become mewhen was Tricksy here?

LATELY - Yesterday, Maam, with her Bill.

MRS MODERN - How! her Bill already?

LATELY - She says, Maam, your Ladyship bid her bring it.

MRS MODERN - Ay, to be sure, she'll not fail to remember that.

LATELY - She says too, Maam, that she's in great Distress for her Money.

MRS MODERN - Oh, no doubt of that, I do not know any one who is not.

LATELY - What shall I do, Maam, when she comes again?

MRS MODERN - You mustyou must send her away again, I think.

LATELY - Yes, Maam, but

MRS MODERN - But—but what? don't trouble me with your Impertinence, I have other things to think on—Bills! Bills! Bills! I wonder, in a civiliz'd Nation, there are no Laws against Duns. [Knocking at the Door.] Come in.

SCENE II

To them Footman.

FOOTMAN - My Lady Ever–play, Madam, gives her humble Service to you, and desires your Ladyship's Company To–morrow Se'nnight to make a Party at Quadrille with my Lady Lose–all, and Mrs. Banespouse.

MRS MODERN - Lately, bring the Quadrille Book hither, see whether I am engag'd.

LATELY - Here it is, Maam.

MRS MODERN - Run over the Engagements.

LATELY - Monday, February 5. at Mrs. Squabble's; Tuesday, at Mrs. Witless's; Wensday, at Lady Matadore's; Thursday , at Mrs. Fiddle–Faddle's; Friday, at Mrs. Ruin's; Saturday , at Lady Trifle's; Sunday, at Lady Barbara Pawnjewels.

MRS MODERN - What is the Wench doing?—see for how long I am engag'd—at this rate you will not have done this Hour.

LATELY - Maam, your Ladyship is engag'd ev'ry Night till Thursday three Weeks.

MRS MODERN - My Service to Lady Ever–play, I have Parties ev'ry Night till Thursday three Weeks, and then I shall be very glad if she will get two more at my House and Tom—take the Roll of Visits, and go with my Chair to pay them, but remember not to call at Mrs. Worthy's.

SCENE III

MRS MODERN - Lately, I intend to leave off her Acquaintance, for I never see any People of Fashion at her House; which, indeed, I do not wonder at, for the Wretch is hardly ever to be found without her Husband. And truly, I think, she is not fit Company for any other. Did you ever see any one dress like her, Lately?

LATELY - Oh, frightful! I have wonder'd how your Laship cou'd endure her so long.

MRS MODERN - Why, she plays at Quadrille worse than she dresses, and one wou'd endure a great deal in a Person who loses her Money.

LATELY - Nay, now I wonder that your Laship has left her off at all.

MRS MODERN - Truly, because she has left off Play; and now she rails at Cards for the same Reason, as some Women do at Gallantry from ill Success. Poor Creatures! how ignorant they are, that all their railing is only a loud Proclamation, that they have lost their Money, or a Lover!

LATELY - They may rail as long as they please, Maam, they will never be able to expel those two Pleasures out of the World.

MRS MODERN - Ah, Lately! I hope, I shall be expell'd out of the World first. Those Quadrille Rings of mine are worth more Money, than four of the best Brilliants. There is more Conjuration in these dear Circles; [Shews a Ring.] These Spades, Hearts, Clubs and Diamonds. Heark, I hear my Husband coming, go you down Stairs.

[Exit Lately]
Husband, did I say? Sure, the Wretch, who sells his Wife, deserves another Name; but I must be civil to him while I despise him.

SCENE IV

Mr. Modern, Mrs Modern

MRS MODERN - My Dear, Good-morrow.

MR MODERN - I hope, you slept well last Night, Madam; that is, I hope, you had good Success at Cards.

MRS MODERN - Very indifferent. I had won a considerable Sum if it had not been for a cursed Sans-prendre-vole, that swept the whole Table. That Lady Weldon has such Luck, if I were superstitious, I shou'd forswear playing with her for I never play'd with her, but I cheated, nor ever play'd with her, but I lost.

MR MODERN - Then without being very superstitious, I think, you may suspect that she cheats too.

MRS MODERN - Did I not know the other Company; for the very worst of Quadrille is, one cannot cheat without a Partner. The Division of a Booty gives one more Pain, than the winning it can Pleasure I am to make up Accounts to-morrow with Mrs. Sharpring but where to get the Money, I know not, unless you have it, Child.

MR MODERN - I have it! I wanted to borrow some of you; unless you can raise me 500 Pounds by tomorrow Night, I shall be in a fair way to go to Jail the next Morning.

MRS MODERN - If the whole Happiness of my Life depended on it, I cou'd not get the tenth part.

MR MODERN - You do not manage Lord Richly right: Men will give any thing to a Woman they are fond of.

MRS MODERN - But not to a Woman whom they were fond of The Decay of Lord Richly's Passion is too apparent for you not to have observ'd it. He visits me seldom, and I am afraid, shou'd I ask a Favour of him, it might break off our Acquaintance.

MR MODERN - Then, I see no reason for your Acquaintance; he dances no longer at my House, if he will not pay the Musick. But hold, I have a Thought come into my Head, may oblige him to it, and make better Musick for us than you imagine.

MRS MODERN - What is it?

MR MODERN - Suppose, I procur'd Witnesses of his Familiarity with youI shou'd recover swinging Damages.

MRS MODERN - But then my Reputation

MR MODERN - Pooh, you will have enough to gild it; never fear your Reputation, while you are rich for Gold in this World covers as many Sins, as Charity in the next. So that get a great deal, and give away a little, and you secure your Happiness in both. Besides, in this Case, all the Scandal falls on the Husband.

MRS MODERN - Oh no! I shall be no more visitedFarewel, dear Quadrille ; dear, dear, Sans, prendre, vole, and Matadores.

MR MODERN - You will be forc'd to quit these Pleasures otherwise, for your Companions in 'em will quit you the very Moment they apprehend our sinking Fortune. You will find that Wealth has a surer Interest to introduce Roguery into Company, than Vertue to introduce Poverty.

MRS MODERN - You will never persuade me: my Reputation is dearer to me than my Life.

MR MODERN - Very strange, that a Woman who made so little Scruple of sacrificing the Substance of her Vertue, shou'd make so much of parting with the Shadow of it.

MRS MODERN - 'Tis the Shadow only that is valuableReputation is the Soul of Vertue.

MR MODERN - So far indeed, that it survives long after the Body is dead. Tho' to me, Vertue has appeared nothing more than a Sound, and Reputation is its Echo. Is there not more Charm in the Chink of a thousand Guineas, than in ten thousand Praises? But what need more Arguments, as I have been contented to wear Horns for your Pleasure, it is but reasonable, you shou'd let me show 'em for my Profit.

MRS MODERN - If my Pleasures, Mr. Modern, had been your only Inducement, you wou'd have acted another Part. How have you maintain'd your Figure in the World since your Losses in the South–Sea, and others? and do you upbraid me with the Crimes which you your self have licens'd have liv'd by?

MR MODERN - Had I follow'd my own Inclinations, I had retir'd; and instead of supporting these Extravagances by such Methods, had reduc'd my Pleasures to my Fortune. 'Twas you, Madam, who by your unbridl'd Pride, and Vanity run me into Debt, and thenI gave up your Person to secure my own.

MRS MODERN - Ha! have I secur'd thy worthless Person at the Expence of mine? no, Wretch, 'tis at the Price of thy Shame, I have purchas'd Pleasures. Why, why do I say thy Shame? the mean, the groveling Animal, whom any fear cou'd force to render up the Honour of his Wife, must be above the fear of Shame. Did I not come unblemisht to thee? Was not my Life unspotted as my Fame, 'till at thy base Intreaties I gave up my Innocence?Oh! that I had sooner seen thee starve in Prison, which yet I will, ere thou shalt reap the Fruits of my Misfortunes. No, I will publish thy Dishonour to the World.

MR MODERN - Nay, but, my Dear.

MRS MODERN - Despicable Monster!

MR MODERN - But, Child, hearken to Reason.

MRS MODERN - Never, never.

MR MODERN - I own my self in the wrong. I ask ten thousand Pardons. I will submit to any Punishment.

MRS MODERN - To upbraid me with

MR MODERN - My Dear, I am in the wrong, I say: I never will be guilty of the like again.

MRS MODERN - Leave me a while, perhaps, I may come to my self.

MR MODERN - My Dear, I am obedient. Sure, the Grand Seignior has no Slave equal to a contented Cuckold.

[Exit.

SCENE V

Mrs. Modern alone.

MRS MODERN - What shall I do? Money must be rais'dbut how? Is there on Earth a Person that wou'd lend me twenty Guineas! I have lost Gaywit's Heart too long to expect any thing there, nor wou'd my Love ever suffer me to ask him. Ha! Bellamant, perhaps may do it: he is generous, and I believe, he loves me. I will try him, however What wretched Shifts are they oblig'd to make use of, who wou'd support the Appearance of a Fortune which they have not!

[Exit.

SCENE VI

The Street before Lord Richly's Door. Capt Merit

CAPT MERIT - That is the Door I must attack, and I have attackt a City with less Reluctance. There is more Hardship in one Hour's base Solicitation at a Levée, than in a whole Campaign.

SCENE VII

Capt Merit, Porter.

CAPT MERIT -
Does my Lord Richly see Company this Morning?

PORTER - Sir, I cannot tell yet, whether he does or no.

CAPT MERIT - Nay, I have seen several Gentlemen go in.

PORTER - I know not whom you may see go in. I suppose, they have Business with his Lordship. I hope, you will give my Lord leave to be at home to whom he pleases.

CAPT MERIT - If Business be a Passport to his Lordship, I have Business with him of Consequence.

PORTER - Sir, I shall tell him of it.

CAPT MERIT - Sir, I shall be oblig'd to you, to tell him now.

PORTER - I cannot carry any Message now, unless I knew you.

CAPT MERIT - Why, don't you know me? that my Name is Merit.

PORTER - Sir, here are so many Gentlemen come ev'ry Day, that unless I have often new Tokens to remember 'em by, it is impossibleStand by there, room for my Lord Lazy.

[Lord Lazy crosses in a Chair.

SCENE VIII

Capt Merit, Capt Bravemore, from the House.

CAPT BRAVEMORE - Merit, Good morrow; what important Affair can have sent you hither, whom I know to shun the Houses of the Great, as much as Vertue does?

CAPT MERIT - Or as much as they do Poverty, for I have not been able to advance farther than you see me. 'Sdeath, I have mounted a Breach against an armed File of the Enemy, and yet a single Porter has deny'd me Entrance at that Door. You, I see, have speeded better.

CAPT BRAVEMORE - Ha! ha! ha! thou errant Man of Warhark'ye, Friend, there is but one Key to all the great Mens Houses in Town.

CAPT MERIT - Is it not enough to cringe to Pow'r, but we must do the same to the Servants of Pow'r?

CAPT BRAVEMORE - Sir, the Servants of a great Man are all great Men. Wou'd you get within their Doors, you must bow to the Porter, and Fee him too. Then to go farther, you must pay your Devoirs to his Gentleman; and after you have bowed for about half an Hour to his whole Family, at last you may get a Bow from himself.

CAPT MERIT - Damnation! I'd sooner be a Galley–Slave; shall I, who have spent my Youth and Health in my Country's Service, be forc'd by such mean Vassalage to defend my old Age from Cold and Hunger, while ev'ry painted Butterfly wantons in the Sunshine? [Colonel Courtly crosses.] 'Sdeath, there's a Fellow nowthat Fellow's Father was a Pimp; his Mother, she turn'd Bawd; and his Sister, turn'd Whore; you see the Consequence: How happy is that Country, where pimping and whoring are esteemed publick Services, and where Grandeur, and the Gallows lie on the same Road!

CAPT BRAVEMORE - But leaving off railing, what is your Business with his Lordship?

CAPT MERIT - There is a Company vacant in Colonel Favourite's Regiment, which by his Lordship's Interest I hope to gain.

CAPT BRAVEMORE - But pray, by what do you hope to gain his Lordship's Interest?

CAPT MERIT - You know, Bravemore, I am little inclin'd to boasting; but I think, my Services may speak something for me.

CAPT BRAVEMORE - Faith, I'm afraid you will find 'em dumb; or if they do speak, it will be a Language understood by the Great. Suppose you apply to his Nephew, Mr. Gaywit; His Interest with my Lord, may be of service to you.

CAPT MERIT - I have often seen him at Mr. Bellamont's, and believe he wou'd do any thing to serve me.

CAPT BRAVEMORE - But the Levee is begun by this: if you please, I'll introduce you to't.

CAPT MERIT - What an abundance of poor Wretches go to the feeding the Vanity of that Leviathan one great Rogue.

SCENE IX

Lord Richly at his House.

LORD RICHLY - Ha! ha! Ha agreeable! Courtly, thou art the greatest Droll upon Earth you'll dine with meLord Lazy, will you make me happy too?

LORD LAZY - I'll make my self so, my Lord.

LORD RICHLY - Mr. Woodall, your Servant, how long have you been in Town?

WOODALL - I cannot be particular, I carry no Almanack about me, my Lord, a Week or a Fortnight perhaps, too much time to lose at this Season, when a Man shou'd be driving the Foxes out of his Country.

COLONEL COURTLY - I hope, you have brought your Family to Town; a Parliament–man shou'd always bring his Wife with him, that if he does not serve the Publick, she may.

LORD RICHLY - Now I think Familiarity with the Wife of a Senator shou'd be made a Breach of Privilege.

COLONEL COURTLY - Your Lordship is in the rightthe Person of his Wife shou'd be made as sacred as his own.

WOODALL - Ay, the Women wou'd thank us damnably for such a Vote and the Colonel here is a very likely Man to move it.

COLONEL COURTLY - Not I, for the Women then wou'd be as backward to be our Wives, as the Tradesmen are now to be our Creditors.

WOODALL - To the fine Gentlemen of us, who lay out their small Fortunes in Extravagance, and their slender Stock of Love on their Wenches. I remember the time, when I was a young Fellow, that Men us'd to dress like Men: But now I meet with nothing but a Parcel of Toupet Coxcombs, who plaister up their Brains upon their Periwigs.

LORD RICHLY - I protest thou art an errant Wit, Woodall

COLONEL COURTLY - Oh, he's one of the greatest Wits of his County.

WOODALL - I have one of the greatest Estates of my County, and by what I can see, that entitles a Man to Wit here, as well as there.

CAPT MERIT - Methinks, this rough Spark is very free with his Lordship.
[To Bravemore.

CAPT BRAVEMORE - You must know, this is a sort of polite Bear–baiting. There is hardly a great Man in Town but what is fond of these sort of Fellows; whom they take a delight in baiting with one or more Buffoons. But now for your Business.

LORD RICHLY - I shall see him this Morning; you may depend on my speaking about it. Captain Bravemore, I am glad to see you.

[To a Gentleman.

CAPT BRAVEMORE - My Lord, here is a Gentleman of distinguish'd Services. If your Lordship wou'd recommend him to Colonel Favourite.

LORD RICHLY - Sir, I shall certainly do it.

CAPT MERIT - There being a Company vacant, my Lordmy Name is Merit.

LORD RICHLY - Mr. Merit, I shall be extremely glad to serve you. Sir John, your most obedient humble Servant Lazy, what were you saying about Mr. Bellamant?

LORD LAZY - We were talking, my Lord, of his Affair, which was heard in our House yesterday.

LORD RICHLY - I am sorry I was not there. It went against him, I think.

LORD LAZY - Yes, my Lord, and I am afraid it affects him deeply.

COLONEL COURTLY - Undone, Sir, quite undone.

LORD RICHLY - Upon my Soul, Mrs. Bellamant's a fine Woman.

WOODALL - Then I suppose, if her Husband's undone, you'll have her among you.

LORD RICHLY - Woodall, thour't a Liquorish Dog. Thou woud'st have the first Snap.

WOODALL - Not I, none of your Town Ladies for me; I always take leave of Women from the time I come out of the Country till I go back agen.

LORD LAZY - Women! Pox on him! he means Foxes agen.

COLONEL COURTLY - He knows no difference.

WOODALL - Nor you either; but, hark'e, I fancy it is safer riding after the one, than the other.

COLONEL COURTLY - Thy Ideas are as gross as thy Person.

LORD RICHLY - Hang him, sly Rogueyou never knew a Fox-hunter, that did not love a Wench.

WOODALL - No, nor a Wench of any Sense that did not love a Fox-hunter.

LORD RICHLY - Modern, your Servant.

MR MODERN - I would presume only to remind your Lordship

LORD RICHLY - Depend upon it, I will remember youI hope, your Lady is well.

MR MODERN - Entirely at your Service, my Lord.

LORD RICHLY - I have a particular Affair to communicate to her, a Secret that I cannot send by you; you know, all Secrets are not proper to trust a Husband with.

MR MODERN - You do her too much Honour, my Lord; I believe you will find her at Home any time to-day.

LORD RICHLY - Faith, Modern, I know not whether thou art happier in thy Temper, or in thy Wife.

MR MODERN - Ummy Lord, as for my Wife, I believe, she is as good as most Wives, I believe she is a vertuous Woman; that I think I may affirm of her.

LORD RICHLY - That thou may'st, I dare swear; and that I as firmly believe as thou dost thy self; and let me tell you, a virtuous Woman is no common Jewel in this Agebut prithee, hast thou heard any thing of Mr. Bellamant's Affairs?

MR MODERN - No more, than that he has lost his Cause, which he seem'd to expect the other Night, when he was at my House.

LORD RICHLY - Then you are intimate.

MR MODERN - He visits my Wife pretty often, my Lord.

LORD RICHLY - Modern, you know I am your Friendand now we are alone let me advise you. Take care of Bellamant, take a particular care of Bellamant he is prudent enough in his Amours to pass upon the World for a Constant Husband; but I know himI know himhe is a dangerous Man.

MR MODERN - My Lord, you surprize me so that

LORD RICHLY - I know you will excuse this Freedom my Friendship takes; but beware of Bellamant as you love your Honour.

SERVANT - My Lord, the Coach is at the Door.

LORD RICHLY - My dear Modern, I see the great Surprize you are in: but you'll excuse my Freedom.

MR MODERN - I am eternally oblig'd to your Lordship

LORD RICHLY - Your humble Servant.

MR MODERN - I hope your Lordship will pardon my Freedom, if after all these Obligations I beg leave once more to remind you.

LORD RICHLY - Depend upon it, I'll take care of you. What a World of poor chimerical Devils does a Levee draw together? All gaping for Favours, without the least Capacity of making a Return for them. But great Men justly act, by wiser Rules; A Levee is the Paradise of Fools.

ACT II

SCENE I

SCENE Mrs. Bellamant's House.

Mrs. Bellamant, Emilia

MRS BELLAMANT - Bid John put up the Coach. [To a Servant.] What think you now, Emilia? has not this Morning's Ramble giv'n you a Surfeit of the Town? After all the Nonsense and Ill-nature we have heard to-day, wou'd it grieve one to part with the Place one is sure to hear 'em over again in?

EMILIA - I am far from thinking any of its Pleasures worth too eager a Wish and the Woman who has with her, in the Country, the Man she loves, must be a very ridiculous Creature to pine after the Town.

MRS BELLAMANT - And yet, my Dear, I believe you know there are such ridiculous Creatures.

EMILIA - I rather imagine, they retire with the Man they shou'd love, than him they do: For a Heart that is passionately fond of the Pleasures here, has rarely room for any other Fondness. The Town it self is the Passion of the greater Part of our Sex; But such I can never allow a just Notion of Love toA Woman, that sincerely loves, can know no Happiness without, nor Misery with her beloved Object.

MRS BELLAMANT - You talk feelingly, I protest, I wish you don't leave your Heart behind you Come, confess; I hope, I have deserv'd rather to be esteem'd your Confident than your Mother-in-Law.

EMILIA - Wou'd it be a Crime, if it were so? But if Love be a Crime, I am sure you cannot upbraid me with it.

MRS BELLAMANT - Tho' if it be a Crime, I am sure you are guilty. Well, I approve your Choice, Child.

EMILIA - My Choice! Excellent! I carry his Picture in my Eyes, I suppose.

MRS BELLAMANT - As sure as in your Heart, my Dear.

EMILIA - Nay, but dear Madam, tell me whom you guess.

MRS BELLAMANT - Hush, here's Mr. Bellamant.

Enter Bellamant.

MR BELLAMANT - So soon return'd, my Dear? Sure, you found no Body at Home.

MRS BELLAMANT - Oh, my Dear! I have been in such an Assembly of Company, and so pulled to pieces with Impertinence and Ill-nature. Welcome, Welcome! the Country! for sure the World is so very bad, those Places are best, where one has the least of it.

MR BELLAMANT - What's the Matter?

MRS BELLAMANT - In short, I have been downright affronted.

MR BELLAMANT - Who durst affront you?

MRS BELLAMANT - A Set of Women that dare do ev'ry thing, but what they shou'd doIn the first Place, I was complimented with Prude, for not being at the last Masqueradewith Dulness, for not entring into the Taste of the Town in some of its DiversionsThen had my whole Dress run over, and dislik'd; and to finish all, Mrs. Termagant told me I lookt frightful.

MR BELLAMANT - Not all the Paint in Italy can give her half your Beauty.

MRS BELLAMANT - You are certainly the most complaisant Man in the World, and I the only Wife who can retire Home, to be put in a good Humour. Most Husbands are like a plain-dealing Looking-glass, which sullies all the Compliments we have receiv'd abroad, by assuring us we do not deserve 'em.

[During this Speech a Servant delivers a Letter to Bellamant, which he reads.

EMILIA - I believe tho', Madam, that generally happens when they are not deserv'd: for a Woman of true Beauty can never feel any Dissatisfaction from the Justice of her Glass; nor she, who has your Worth, from the Sincerity of Her Husband.

MRS BELLAMANT - Your Father seems discompos'dI wish there be no ill News in his Letter.

MR BELLAMANT - My Dear, I have a Favour to ask of you.

MRS BELLAMANT - Say to command me.

MR BELLAMANT - I gave you a Bank Note of a Hundred Yesterday, you must let me have it agen.

MRS BELLAMANT - I am the luckiest Creature in the World, that I did not pay away some of it this Morning. Emilia, Child, come with me.

[Exit with Emilia

MR BELLAMANT - Excellent! Unhappy Woman! How little doth she guess, she fetches this Money for a Rival? That is all the little Merit I can boast towards her. To have contended by the utmost Civility and Compliance, with all her Desires, and the utmost Caution in the Management of my Amour, to disguise from her a Secret, that must have made her miserable. Let me read once more.

SIR, If you have, or ever had any Value for me, send me a Hundred Pounds this Morning, or to make 'em more welcome than the last of Necessities can, bring them your self to. Yours more than her own, Hillaria Modern. Why, what a Farce is human Life? How ridiculous is the Pursuit of our Desires, when the Enjoyment of 'em is sure to beget new ones?

SCENE IV

Mr. Bellamant, Cap. Bellamant.

CAPT BELLAMANT - Good-morrow, Sir.

MR BELLAMANT - I suppose, Sir, by the Gaiety of your Dress, and your Countenance, I may wish you Joy of something besides your
Father's Misfortunes.

CAPT BELLAMANT - Wou'd you have me go into Mourning for your Losses, Sir?

MR BELLAMANT - You may mourn, Sir I am now unable to support your Extravagance any longer. My Advice, nay, my Commands have had no Effect upon you, but Necessity must; and your Extravagance must fall of Course, when it has nothing to support it.

CAPT BELLAMANT - I am surpriz'd you shou'd call the Expences of a Gentleman, Extravagance.

MR BELLAMANT - I am sorry you think the Expences of a Fool, or Fop, the Expences of a Gentleman: and that Race-Horses, Cards, Dice, Whores, and Embroidery are necessary Ingredients in that amiable Composition.

CAPT BELLAMANT - Faith, and they are so with most Gentlemen of my Acquaintance; and give me leave to tell you, Sir, these are the Qualifications which recommend a Man to the best Sort of People. Suppose, I had staid at the University, and follow'd Greek and Latin, as you advis'd me; What Acquaintance had I found at Court? What Bows had I receiv'd at an Assembly, or the Opera?

MR BELLAMANT - And will you please to tell me, Sir, what Advantage you have receiv'd from these? Are you the wiser, or the richer? What are you? Why, in your Opinion, better drest. Where else had been that smart Toupet, that elegant Sword–knot, that Coat cover'd with Lace, and then with Powder? That ever Heav'n shou'd make me Father to such a drest up Daw! A Creature, who draws all his Vanity from the Gifts of Tailors, and Periwig–Makers!

CAPT BELLAMANT - Wou'd you not have your Son drest, Sir?

MR BELLAMANT - Yes, and, if he can afford it, let him be sometimes fine; but let him dress like a Man, not affect the Woman, in his Habit, or his Gesture.

CAPT BELLAMANT - If a Man will keep good Company, he must comply with the Fashion.

MR BELLAMANT - I would no more comply with a ridiculous Fashion, than with a vicious one; nor with that which makes a Man look like a Monkey, than that which makes him act like any other Beast.

CAPT BELLAMANT - Lord, Sir! you are grown strangely unpolite.

MR BELLAMANT - I shall not give my self any farther Trouble with you: But since all my Endeavours have prov'd ineffectualleave you to the Bent of your own Inclinations. But I must desire you to send me no more Bills; I assure you, I shall not answer themyou must live on your Commissionthis last Misfortune has made it impossible that I shou'd add one Farthing to your Income.

CAPT BELLAMANT - I have an Affair in my View, which may add to itSir, I wish you Good–morrowwhen a Father and Son must not talk of Money–Matters, I cannot see what they have to do together.

SCENE V

Mr. Bellamant, Mrs. Bellamant, Emilia

MRS BELLAMANT - Here is the Bill, my Dear.

MR BELLAMANT - You shall be repaid in a Day or two.

MRS BELLAMANT - I saw your Son part hastily from you, as I came in; I hope, you have not been angry with him.

MR BELLAMANT - Why will you ever intermeddle between us?

MRS BELLAMANT - I hope you will pardon an Intercession, my Dear, for a Son–in–Law; which I shou'd not be guilty of for a Son of my own.

SCENE VI

Mr. Gaywit, Mr. Bellamant, Mrs. Bellamant, Emilia

MR GAYWIT - Bellamant, Good–morrowLadies, your humble Servant.

MR BELLAMANT - Servant, Mr Gaywit I thought your time had been so employ'd, that you had forgot your Friends.

MR GAYWIT - I ought to excuse so long an Absence, but as Bellamant knows that it must give my self the greatest Pain, he will impute it to Business.

MR BELLAMANT - Did I not also know, that two Days of thy Life were never giv'n to Business yet?

MR GAYWIT - Not what the grave World call so, I confess; but of what the gay World allow that Name to, no Hands were ever fuller.

MR BELLAMANT - You have been making Love to some new Mistress, I suppose.

MR GAYWIT - Fy, it is only Husbands make a Business of Love, to us 'tis but an Amusement.

MRS BELLAMANT - Very fine! and to my Face too!

MR GAYWIT - Mr. Bellamant, Madam, is so known an Exception to the general Mode of Husbands, that what is thrown on them, cannot effect one of so celebrated a Constancy.

MRS BELLAMANT - That's a Virtue he may be celebrated for, without much Envy.

MR GAYWIT - He will be envy'd by all Men, for the Cause of that Constancy. Were such Wives as Mrs. Bellamant less scarce, such Husbands as my Friend wou'd be more common.

EMILIA - You are always throwing the Fault on us.

MRS BELLAMANT - It is commonly in us, either in our Choice of our Husband, or our Behaviour to them. No Woman, who married a Man of perfect Sense, was ever unhappy, but from her own Folly. [Knock here.

MR GAYWIT - [Looking out of the Window.]
Ha! a very worthy Uncle of mine, my Lord Richly.

MR BELLAMANT - You'll excuse me, if I am not at Home.

MR GAYWIT - Fy! to deny your self to him, wou'd be unprecedented.

MR BELLAMANT - I assure you, no—for I have often done it.

MR GAYWIT - Then, I believe, you are the only Man in Town that has. But it is too late, I hear him on the Stairs.

MRS BELLAMANT - Come, Emilia, we'll leave the Gentlemen to their Entertainment; I have been surfeited with it already.

SCENE VII

Lord Richly, Mr. Gaywit, Mr. Bellamant.

LORD RICHLY - Dear Bellamant, I am your most obedient Servant. I am come to ask you ten thousand Pardons, that my Affairs prevented my Attendance the Day your Cause came on. It might have been in my Power to have serv'd you beyond my single Vote.

MR BELLAMANT - I am oblig'd to your Lordship, but as I have great Reason to be satisfied with the Justice of your honourable House I am contented.

LORD RICHLY - I hope, the Loss was not considerable.

MR BELLAMANT - I thought your Lordship had heard.

LORD RICHLY - I think, I was told twenty thousand Pound but that's a Trifle, a small Retrenchment in one's Expences two or three dozen Suits the less, and two or three dozen fewer Women in a Year, will soon reimburse you.

MR BELLAMANT - My Loss is not equal to what your Lordship intimates; nor can I complain of a Fortune, still large enough to retire into the Country with.

LORD RICHLY - Nay, dear Bellamant, we must not lose you so. Have you no Friend that cou'd favour you with some comfortable snug Employment, of a thousand or fifteen Hundred per Annum?

MR GAYWIT - Your Lordship is the properest Person in the World.

LORD RICHLY - Who I? I am sure, no Mortal wou'd do half so much to serve dear Jack Bellamant as my self but I have no Interest in the least.

MR BELLAMANT - I am oblig'd to the good Offices of my Friend, but I assure your Lordship I have no Intention that way. Besides, I have liv'd long enough in the World, to see that Necessity is a bad a Recommendation to Favours of that kind, which as seldom fall to those who really want them, as to those who really deserve them.

LORD RICHLY - I can't help saying, those things are not easily obtained. I heartily wish I could serve you in any thing. It gives me a great deal of Uneasiness that my Power is not equal to my Desire. Damn it, I must turn this Discourse, or he'll never have done with it. Oh, Bellamant! have you heard of the new Opera of Mr. Crambo?

MR GAYWIT - What's the Name of it?

LORD RICHLY - It will be call'd the Humours of Bedlam. I have read it, and it is a most surprizing fine Performance. It has not one Syllable of Sense in it from the first Page to the last.

MR GAYWIT - It must certainly take.

LORD RICHLY - Sir, it shall take, if I have Interest enough to support it. I hate your dull Writers of the late Reigns. The Design of a Play is to make you laugh; and who can laugh at Sense?

MR GAYWIT - I think, my Lord, we have improv'd on the Italians. They wanted only Sense We have neither Sense, nor Musick.

LORD RICHLY - I hate all Musick but a Jig.

MR GAYWIT - I don't think it wou'd be an ill Project, my Lord, to turn the best of our Tragedies and Comedies into Operas.

LORD RICHLY - And, instead of a Company of Players, I wou'd have a Company of Tumblers and Ballad–Singers.

MR BELLAMANT - Why, Faith, I believe it will come to that soon, unless some sturdy Critick should oppose it.

LORD RICHLY - No Critick shall oppose it. It wou'd be very fine, truly, if Men of Quality were confin'd in their Taste; we should be rarely diverted, if a Set of Pedants were to licence all our Diversions; the Stage then wou'd be as dull as a Country Pulpit.

MR GAYWIT - And the Boxes in Drury–Lane, as empty as the Galleries in St. James's.

MR BELLAMANT - Like enough: for Religion and common Sense are in a fair way to be banish'd out of the World together.

LORD RICHLY - Let 'em go, egad.

MR BELLAMANT - This is, I believe, the only Age that has scorn'd a Pretence to Religion.

LORD RICHLY - Then it is the only Age that hath scorn'd Hypocrisy.

MR BELLAMANT - Rather, that Hypocrisy is the only Hypocrisy it wants. You shall have a known Rascal set up for Honoura Fool for Witand your professed dear bosom fawning Friend, who, tho' he wallow in Wealth, wou'd refuse you ten Guineas to preserve you from Ruin, shall lose a hundred times that Sum at Cards, to ruin your Wife.

LORD RICHLY - There dear Jack Bellamant is the happiest Man in the World, by possessing a Wife whom a thousand times that Sum wou'd have no effect on.

MR BELLAMANT - I look upon my self equally happy, my Lord, in having no such Friend as wou'd tempt her.

LORD RICHLY - That thou hast not, I dare swear. But I thank you for putting me in mind of it. I must engage her in my Author's Cause, for I know her Judgment has a great Sway.

MR BELLAMANT - As our Stay will be so short in Town, she can do you no Service; besides, I have heard her detest Partiality in those Affairs; you wou'd never persuade her to give a Vote contrary to her Opinion.

LORD RICHLY - Detest Partiality! ha, ha, haI have heard a Lady declare for doing Justice to a Play, and condemn it the very next MinuteTho' I knew she had neither seen, nor read it. Those things are entirely guided by Favour.

MR GAYWIT - Nay, I see no reason to fix the Scandal on the Ladies; Party and Prejudice have the same Dominion over us. Ask a Man's Character of one of his Party, and you shall hear he is one of the worthiest, honestest Fellows in Christendom; ask it of one of the opposite Party, and you shall find him as worthless, good-for-nothing a Dog as ever was hang'd.

MR BELLAMANT - So that a Man must labour very hard to get a general good Reputation, or a general bad one.

LORD RICHLY - Well, since you allow so much, you will give me leave to tempt Mrs. Bellamant.

MR BELLAMANT - With all my Heart, my Lord.

MR GAYWIT - Thou art a well-bred Husband, indeed, to give another leave to tempt your Wife.

MR BELLAMANT - I shou'd have been a very ill-bred one to have deny'd it. Who's there?

Enter Servant.

LORD RICHLY - If I had said more, he had granted it, rather than have lost my Favour. Poverty makes as many Cuckolds as it does Thieves.

[Aside.

MR BELLAMANT - Wait on my Lord Richly to your Mistress's ApartmentI am your most obedient Servant.

SCENE VIII

Mr. Gaywit, Mr. Bellamant.

MR GAYWIT - I find, you are resolv'd to make your Wife share your Misfortunes. It wou'd have been civil to have giv'n her the Choice of not being at Home.

MR BELLAMANT - I wanted to be alone with youbesides, Women have a Liberty of sending away an impertinent Visitant which we have not.

MR GAYWIT - Ay, and a Way of entertaining Visitants too which we have not; and he is a Visitant not easily sent away, I assure you. I have known him receive very vigorous Rebuffs without retreating.

MR BELLAMANT - You talk as if you suspected his making Love to my Wife.

MR GAYWIT - He does so to every Woman he sees; neither the strictest Friendship profess'd to her Husband, nor the best Reputation on her own side, can preserve any Woman he likes from his Attacks: for he is arriv'd at a happy way of regarding all the rest of Mankind as his Tenants, and thinks because he possesses more than they, he is entitled to whatever they possess.

MR BELLAMANT - Insolent Vanity! I wonder the Spirit of Mankind has not long since crush'd the Tyranny of such Lordly Wolves; yet believe me, Gaywit, there generally goes a great deal of Affectation to compose this voluptuous Man. He ofter injures Women in their Fame, than in their Persons. This Affectation of Variety discovers a sickly Appetite; and many Mistresses, like many Dishes, are often sent away untasted.

MR GAYWIT - A very innocent Affectation truly, to destroy a Lady's Fame.

MR BELLAMANT - Why ay, for we are come to an Age, wherein a Woman may live very comfortably without it: as long as the Husband is content with his Infamy, the Wife escapes hers.

MR GAYWIT - And I am mistaken, if many Husbands in this Town do not live very comfortably by being content with their Infamy, nay, by being Promoters of it. It is a modern Trade, unknown to our Ancestors, a modern Bubble, which seems to be in a rising Condition at present.

MR BELLAMANT - It is a Stock−jobbing Age, ev'ry thing has its Price; Marriage is Traffick throughout; as most of us bargain to be Husbands, so some of us bargain to be Cuckolds; and he wou'd be as much laught at, who preferr'd his Love to his Interest, at this End of the Town, as he who preferr'd his Honesty to his Interest at the other.

MR GAYWIT - You, Bellamant, have had Boldness enough, in Contradiction to this general Opinion, to choose a Woman from her Sense and Virtues. I wish it were in my Power to follow your Examplebut

MR BELLAMANT - But the Opinion of the World, dear Boy

MR GAYWIT - No, my good Forefathers have chosen a Wife for me. I am oblig'd by the Settlement of Lord Richly's Estate to marry Lady Charlotte.

MR BELLAMANT - How!

MR GAYWIT - The Estate will descend to me so encumber'd, I assure you.

MR BELLAMANT - I thought it had not been in Lord Richly's Power, to have cut off the Entail.

MR GAYWIT - Not if I marry Lady Charlotte.

MR BELLAMANT - I think you are happy in being engag'd to no more disagreeable Woman.

MR GAYWIT - Lady Charlotte, is indeed pretty; but were she ev'ry thing a Lover cou'd wish, or ev'n imaginethere is a Woman, my Friend

MR BELLAMANT - Nay, if you are in Love with another, I pity you.

MR GAYWIT - Did'st thou know how I love, you wou'd pity me: but didst thou know whom, coud'st thou look upon her with Eyes like mine, cou'dst thou behold Beauty, Wit, Sense, Good−nature, contending which shou'd adorn her most?

MR BELLAMANT - Poor Gaywit! thou art gone indeed.

MR GAYWIT - But I suppose, the Ladies have by this discharg'd their Visitant. Now if you please, we will attend them.

MR BELLAMANT - You will excuse me, if I leave you with 'em; which I will not do, unless you promise I shall find you at my return.

MR GAYWIT - I intend to dedicate the Day to your Family; so dispose of me as you please.

Mrs. Modern's House.

Lord Richly, Mrs Modern

MRS MODERN - I think, I ought to blame your UnkindnessI have not seen you so long.

LORD RICHLY - Do you think a Week so long?

MRS MODERN - Once you wou'd have thought so.

LORD RICHLY - Why, truly, Hours in the Spring of Love are something shorter than they are in the Winter.

MRS MODERN - Barbarous Man! do you insult me, after what I have done for you?

LORD RICHLY - I fancy, those Favours have been reciprocal.

MRS MODERN - Have I not giv'n you up my Virtue?

LORD RICHLY - And have I not paid for your Virtue, Madam? I am sure, I am 1500 Pounds out of Pocket, which in my Way of counting, is fourteen more than any Woman's Virtue is worth; in short, our Amour is at an end, for I am in pursuit of another Mistress.

MRS MODERN - Why do you come to torment me with her?

LORD RICHLY - Why, I wou'd have you act like other prudent Women in a lower Station; when you can please no longer with your own Person, e'en do it with other People's.

MRS MODERN - Monster! insupportable!

LORD RICHLY - You may rave, Madam, but if you will not do me a Favour, there are wiser People enow who will I fix'd on you out of a particular Regard to you; for I think, when a Man is to lay out his Money, he is always to do it with his Friends.

MRS MODERN - I'll bear it no longer.

[Going.

LORD RICHLY - Nor I.

[Going.

MRS MODERN - Stay, my Lord, can you be so cruel?

LORD RICHLY - Pshaw!

[Going.

MRS MODERN - Oh! stay! stay! you know my Necessities.

LORD RICHLY - And, I think, I propose a very good Cure for 'em.

MRS MODERN - Lend me a hundred Guineas.

LORD RICHLY - I will do more.

MRS MODERN - Generous Creature!

LORD RICHLY - I'll give you Twenty.

MRS MODERN - Do you jest with my Necessity?

LORD RICHLY - Lookee, Madam, if you will do a good-natur'd Thing for me, I will oblige you in return as I promis'd you before, and I think that very good Payment.

MRS MODERN - Pray, my Lord, use me with Decency at least.

LORD RICHLY - Why should we use more Decency to an old Acquaintance, than you Ladies do to a new Lover, and have more Reason for so doing? You often belye your Hearts, when you use us ill In using you so, we follow the Dictates of our Natures.

Enter a Servant, who delivers a Letter to Mrs Modern

MRS MODERN - Ha! it is Bellamant's Handandthe Note that I desir'dThis is lucky, indeed.

SCENE X

Lord Richly, Mr. Gaywit, Emilia, Lady Charlotte, Captain Bellamant, Mrs Modern

LORD RICHLY - So! here's an end of my Business for the present, I find.

LADY CHARLOTTE - Oh, dear Modern! I am heartily glad to see you are alive; for you must know, I thought it impossible for any one to be alive, and not be at the Rehearsal of the new Opera.

CAPT BELLAMANT - How can you be surpriz'd at one of no Taste, Lady Charlotte?

MRS MODERN - I suppose, it was very full.

LADY CHARLOTTE - Oh! ev'ry Body was there; all the World.

MR GAYWIT - How can that be, Lady Charlotte, when so considerable a Part, as Mrs. Modern, was wanting?

MRS MODERN - Civil Creature! when will you say such a thing?

CAPT BELLAMANT - When I am as dull, Madam.

LORD RICHLY - Very true! no one makes a Compliment, but those that want Wit for Satyr.

MR GAYWIT - Right, my Lord. It is as great a Sign of want of Wit to say a good-natur'd thing, as want of Sense to do one.

LADY CHARLOTTE - Oh! I wou'd not say a good-natur'd thing for the World. Captain Bellamant, did you ever hear me say a good-natur'd thing in your Life?

MR GAYWIT - But I am afraid, Lady Charlotte, tho' Wit be a Sign of Ill-nature, Ill-nature is not always a Sign of Wit.

LADY CHARLOTTE - I'll give you leave to say any thing, after what I have said this MorningOh! dear Modern, I wish, you had seen Emilia's Dressing-box! such Japoning he! he! he! she hath varnished over a Windmil ten several times, before she discover'd, she had placed the wrong Side upwards.

MRS MODERN - I have had just such another Misfortune. I have laid out thirty Pounds on a Chest, and now I dislike it of all things.

LADY CHARLOTTE - Oh! my Dear, I do not like one thing in twenty that I do my self.

EMILIA - You are the only Person that dislikes, I dare say, Lady Charlotte.

LADY CHARLOTTE - Oh, you flatt'ring Creature! I wish, you cou'd bring my Papa to your Opinion. He says, I throw away more Money in Work than in Play.

MRS MODERN - But you have not heard half my Misfortune; for when I sent my Chest to be sold, what do you think I was offer'd for my thirty Pounds worth of Work?

LADY CHARLOTTE - I don't know, fifty Guineas perhaps.

MRS MODERN - Twenty Shillings, as I live.

LADY CHARLOTTE - Oh! intolerable! Oh! insufferable!

CAPT BELLAMANT - But are we to have no Hazard this Morning?

MRS MODERN - With all my HeartLord Richly, what say you?

LORD RICHLY - My Vote always goes with the Majority, Madam.

MRS MODERN - Come then, the Shrine is within, and you that will offer at it, follow me.

SCENE XI

Mr. Gaywit, Emilia

EMILIA - Mr. Gaywit, are you no Gamester?

MR GAYWIT - No, Madam, when I play, 'tis the utmost Stretch of my Complaisance.

EMILIA - I am glad, I can find one who is as great an Enemy to play as my self; for I assure you, we are both of the same Opinion.

MR GAYWIT - I wish we were so in ev'ry thing.

EMILIA - Sir!

MR GAYWIT - I say, Madam, I wish all of my Opinions were as well seconded; and yet, methinks, I wou'd not have your Thoughts the same with mine.

EMILIA - Why so, pray?

MR GAYWIT - Because you must have then many an unhappy Hour, which that you may ever avoid, will be still my heartiest Pray'r.

EMILIA - I am oblig'd to you, Sir.

MR GAYWIT - Indeed, you are not. It is a self–interested Wish: for believe me, to see the least Affliction attend you, wou'd give this Breast the greatest Agony it is capable of feeling.

EMILIA - Nay, this is so extravagant a Flight, I know not what to call it.

MR GAYWIT - Nor Icall it a just Admiration of the highest Worth, call it the tenderest Friendship if you please; tho' much I fear it merits the sweetest, softest Name that can be giv'n to any of our Passions. If there be a Passion pure without Allay, as tender and soft, as violent and strong, you cannot sure miscall it by that Name.

EMILIA - You grow now too philosophical for me to understand you: besides, you wou'd, I am sure, be best understood ironically; for who can believe any thing of Mr. Gaywit, when he hath asserted that he is unhappy?

MR GAYWIT - Nay, I will leave my Case to your own Determination when you know it. Suppose me oblig'd to marry the Woman I don't like, debarr'd for ever from her I love, I dote on, the Delight of my Eyes, the Joy of my Heart. Suppose me oblig'd to forsake her, and marryanother.

EMILIA - But I cannot suppose you oblig'd to that.

MR GAYWIT - Were it not an impertinent Trouble, I cou'd convince you.

EMILIA - I know not why I may not be excus'd a little Concern for one who hath expressed so much for me.

MR GAYWIT - Then, Madam, the Settlement of my whole Fortune obliges me to marry Lady Charlotte Gaywit.

EMILIA - How! but suppose the Refusal were on Lady Charlotte's Side.

MR GAYWIT - That is my only Hope.

EMILIA - And I can assure you, your Hope is not ill-grounded.

MR GAYWIT - I know, she hath express'd some dislike to me; but she is a Woman of that sort, that it is as difficult to be certain of her Dislike, as her Affection; and whom the Prospect of Grandeur wou'd easily make obedient to her Father's Commands.

EMILIA - Well! if you are sincere, I pity you heartily.

MR GAYWIT - And if you are sincere, I never knew Happiness till this dear Moment.

SCENE XII

Mr. Gaywit, Emilia, Lord Richly, Mrs. Modern, Lady Charlotte, Captain Bellamant.

MRS MODERN - Victoria, Victoria!

CAPT BELLAMANT - Stript, by Jupiter!

LADY CHARLOTTE - Eleven Mains together, Modern; you are a Devil.

EMILIA - What's the matter, Lady Charlotte?

LADY CHARLOTTE - Oh, my Dear, you never saw the likeModern has held in nine thousand Mains in one Hand, and won all the World.

MR GAYWIT - She has always great Luck at Hazard.

LORD RICHLY - Surprizing to-day, upon my Word.

MRS MODERN - Surprizing to me; for it is the first Success I have had this Month; and I am sure, my Quadrille makes ev'ry one a sufficient Amends for my Hazard.

LORD RICHLY - You are one of those, whose winning no body ever heard of, or whose losing no one ever saw.

CAPT BELLAMANT - But you forget the Auction, Lady Charlotte.

LADY CHARLOTTE - What have I to do at an Auction, that am ruin'd and undone?

MR GAYWIT - As much as many that are undone; bid out of whim, in order to raise the Price, and ruin others. Or if the Hammer shou'd fall upon you, before you expect it, take a sudden dislike to the Goods, or dispute your own Words, and leave them upon the Hands of the Seller.

MRS MODERN - How polite is that now? Gaywit will grow shortly as well-bred, as Madcap.

CAPT BELLAMANT - We shall have him there too, and he is the life of an Auction.

LADY CHARLOTTE - Oh! the most agreeable Creature in the Worldhe has more Wit than any Body, he has made me laugh five hundred Hours together. Emilia, we will just call there, and then I'll set you down at Home.

EMILIA - Let us but just call then.

LADY CHARLOTTE - That Caution is admirable from you, when you know I never stay above six Minutes any where. Well, you never will reform.

LORD RICHLY - I desire, Charlotte, you wou'd be at Home by Four.

LADY CHARLOTTE - I shall very easily, my Lord, for I have not above fourteen or fifteen Places to call atCome, dear Creature, let us go, for I have more Business than half the World upon my Hands, and I must positively call at the Auction.

MR GAYWIT - Where you have no Business, it seems.

LADY CHARLOTTE - Impertinent! Modern, your Servant.

SCENE XIII

Lord Richly, Mrs Modern

LORD RICHLY - I only waited till you were alone, Madam to renew my Business.

MRS MODERN - If you intend to renew your Impertinence, I wish you wou'd omit both.

LORD RICHLY - So, I find I have my Work to do over again.

MRS MODERN - But if you please, my Lord, to truce with your Proposals, and let Piquet be the Word.

LORD RICHLY - So, you have taken Money out of my Daughters Hands, to put it into mine.

MRS MODERN - Be not confidentI have been too hard for you before now.

LORD RICHLY - Well, and without a Compliment, I know none whom I wou'd sooner lose to than your self; for to any one who loves Play as well as you, and plays as ill, the Money we lose, by a surprizing ill Fortune, is only lent.

MRS MODERN - Methinks, my Lord, you shou'd be fearful of deterring me by this plain-dealing.

LORD RICHLY - I am better acquainted with your Sex. It is as impossible to persuade a Woman that she plays ill, as that she looks ill. The one may make her tear her Cards, and the other break her Looking-glass. Her want of Skill, for want of Luck must pass; As want of Beauty's owing to her Glass.

ACT III

SCENE continues.

Lord Richly, Mrs Modern

MRS MODERN - Can you be so cruel?

LORD RICHLY - Ridiculous! you might as well ask me for my whole Estate; I am sure, I wou'd as soon give it you.

MRS MODERN - An everlasting Curse attend the Cards! to be repiqu'd from forty, when I play'd but for five! my Lord, I believe you a Cheat.

LORD RICHLY - At your Service, Madamwhen you have more Money, if you will honour me with Notice, I will be ready to receive it.

MRS MODERN -
Stay, my Lord give me the twenty Guineas.

LORD RICHLY - On my Conditions.

MRS MODERN - Any Conditions.

LORD RICHLY - Then you must contrive some way or other, a Meeting between me and Mrs. Bellamant, at your House.

MRS MODERN - Mrs. Bellamant!

LORD RICHLY - Why do you start at that Name?

MRS MODERN - She has the Reputation of the strictest Vertue of any Woman in Town.

LORD RICHLY - Virtue! ha, ha, ha! so have you, and so have several of my Acquaintance; there are as few Women who have not the Reputation of Virtue, as that have the thing it self.

MRS MODERN - And what do you propose by meeting her here?

LORD RICHLY - I am too civil to tell you plainly what I propose; tho' by your Question one wou'd imagine you expected it.

MRS MODERN - I expect any thing from you, rather than Civility, my Lord.

LORD RICHLY - Madam, it will be your own Fault, if I am not civil to you. Do this for me, and I'll deny you nothing.

MRS MODERN - There is one thing, which tempts me more than your Gold, which is the Expectation of seeing you desert her, as you have done me.

LORD RICHLY - Which is a Pleasure you'll certainly have; and the sooner you compass my Wishes, the sooner you may triumph in your own: Nay, there is a third Motive will charm thee, my dear Hillaria, more than the other two. When I have laid this Passion, which hath abated that for you, I may return to your Arms with all my former Fondness.

MRS MODERN - Excuse my Incredulity, my Lord; for tho' Love can change its Object, it can never return to the same again.

LORD RICHLY - I may convince you of the contrarybut to our Business; Fortune has declar'd on our Side already, by sending Bellamant hither: cultivate an Acquaintance with him, and you cannot avoid being acquainted with his Wife. She is the perfect Shadow of her Husband; they are as inseparable, as Lady Coquette and her Lapdog.

MRS MODERN - Yes, or as her Ladyship and her Impertinence; or her Lapdog and his Smell. Well, it is to me surprizing, how Women of Fashion can carry Husbands, Children, and Lapdogs about with 'em; three Things I never cou'd be fond of.

LORD RICHLY - If the Ladies were not fonder of their Lapdogs than of their Husbands, we shou'd have no more Dogs in St. James's Parish, than there are Lions at the Tower.

MRS MODERN - It is an uncommon Bravery in you, to single out the Woman who is reputed to be the fondest of her Husband.

LORD RICHLY - She that is fond of one Man, may be fond of another. Fondness, in a Woman's Temper, like the Love of Play, may prefer one Man, and one Game; but will incline her to try more, especially, when she expects greater Profit, and there I am sure, I am superior to my Rival: If Flattery will allure her, or Riches tempt her, she shall be mine; and those are the two great Gates by which the Devil enters the Heart of WomankindPshaw! He here!

SCENE II

Lord Richly, Mr. Modern, Mrs Modern

MR MODERN - I am your Lordship's most obedient humble Servant.

LORD RICHLY - Have you seen this new Opera, Madam?

MRS MODERN - I have heard vast Commendations of it; but I cannot bear an Opera, now poor La Dovi's gone.

LORD RICHLY - Nor I, after poor A la Fama.

MRS MODERN - Oh! Cara la Dovi! I protest, I have often resolv'd to follow her into Italy.

LORD RICHLY - You will allow A la Fama's Voice, I hope.

MRS MODERN - But the Mien of La Dovi, then her Judgment in Singing; the Moment she enter'd the Stage, I have wish'd my self all Eyes.

LORD RICHLY - And the Moment A la Fama sung, I have wish'd my self all Ears.

MR MODERN - I find, I am no desir'd part of this Company. I hope, your Lordship will pardon me; Business of the greatest Consequence requiring my Attendance, prevents my waiting on your Lordship according to my Desires.

Lord Richly, Mrs Modern

LORD RICHLY - This unseasonable Interruption has quite cut the Thread of my Design. Pox on him, a Husband, like the Fool in a Play, is of no Use but to cause Confusion.

MRS MODERN - You wou'd have an Opportunity at my House, and to procure it, I must be acquainted with Mrs. Bellamant; now, there is a lucky Accident which you are not appriz'd ofMr. Bellamant is an humble Servant of mine.

LORD RICHLY - That is lucky indeed; cou'd we give her a Cause of Suspicion that way, it were a lively Prospect of my Success; as persuading a Thief that his Companion is false, is the surest way to make him so.

MRS MODERN - A very pretty Comparison of your Lordship's between the two States.

Enter Servant.

SERVANT - Madam, Mr. Bellamant desires to know, if your Ladyship is at home.

MRS MODERN - I am. Bring him into the Dining–Room.

LORD RICHLY - Thou dear Creature, let me but succeed in this Affair, I'll give thee Millions.

MRS MODERN - More Gold, and fewer Promises, my Lord.

LORD RICHLY - An hundred Guineas shall be the Price of our first Interview.

MRS MODERN - Be punctual, and be confident. Go out the back Way, that he may not see you

LORD RICHLY - Adieu, my Machiavil.

Mrs. Bellamant's House.

Mrs. Bellamant, Mr. Gaywit, Emilia

MRS BELLAMANT - And so, Lady Willitt, after all her Protestations against Matrimony, has at last generously bestowed her self on a young Fellow with no Fortune, the famous Beau Smirk.

EMILIA - She was proof against ev'ry thing but Charity.

MR GAYWIT - To which all other Virtues shou'd be sacrific'd, as it is the greatest; the Ladies are apt to value themselves on their Virtue, as a rich Citizen does on his Purse; and I do not know which is of the greatest Use to the Publick.

MRS BELLAMANT - Nor I, which are the oftnest Bankrupts.

MR GAYWIT - And as, in the City, they suspect a Man who is oftentatious of his Riches; so shou'd I the Woman, who makes the most Noise of her Virtue.

MRS BELLAMANT - We are all the least solicitous about Perfections, which we are well assur'd of our possessing. Flattery is never so agreeable as to our blind Side. Commend a Fool for his Wit, or a Knave for his Honesty, and they will receive you into their Bosoms.

EMILIA - Nay, I have known a pretty Lady who was vain of nothing but her false Locks; and have seen a Pair of squinting Eyes, that never smil'd at a Compliment made to any other Feature.

MR GAYWIT - Yes, Madam, and I know a pretty Gentleman, who obliges me very often with his illspelt Songs; and a very ugly Poet, who hath made me a Present of his Picture.

EMILIA - Well, since you see it is so agreeable to flatter one's blind Side, I think you have no Excuse to compliment on the other.

MR GAYWIT - Then I shall have a very good Excuse to make you no Compliment at all. But this I assure you, Emilia, the first Imperfection I discover, I will tell you of it with the utmost Sincerity.

EMILIA - And I assure you with the utmost Sincerity, I shall not thank you for it.

MRS BELLAMANT - Then without any Flattery, you are two of the most open Plain–dealers I have met with.

SCENE V

Mrs. Bellamant, Emilia, Lady Charotte, Mr Gaywit

LADY CHARLOTTE - Dear Mrs. Bellamant, make some Excuse for me; I see, Emilia is going to chide me for staying so long. When, did she know the Fatigue I had this Afternoon, I was just going into my Coach, when Lady Twitter came in, and forc'd me away to a Fan–shop. Well, I have seen a Set of the prettiest Fans to–day. My dear Creature, where did you get that Lace? I never saw any thing so ravishing.

EMILIA - I cannot see any thing so extraordinary in it.

LADY CHARLOTTE - It cou'd not cost less than ten Pound a YardOh! Mr. Gaywit , are you here?

EMILIA - He goes with us to the Play.

LADY CHARLOTTE - Oh hateful! how can you bear him? I wou'd as soon to the Chappel with Lady Prude: I saw the ridiculous Creature cry at a Tragedy.

MRS BELLAMANT - Do you think he need be asham'd of that, Lady Charlotte?

LADY CHARLOTTE - I wou'd as soon laugh at a Comedy, or fall asleep at an Opera.

MRS BELLAMANT - What is the Play to-night?

LADY CHARLOTTE - I never know that. Miss Rattle and I saw four Acts the other Night, and came away without knowing the Name. I think, one only goes to see the Company, and there will be a great deal to-night; for the Dutchess of Simpleton sent to me this Morning. Emilia , you must go with me after the Play: I must make just fourteen Visits between Nine and Ten: Yesterday, was the first Payment I have made since I came to Town, and I was able to compass no more than three and forty; tho' I only found my Lady Sober at Home, and she was at QuadrilleLud, Mrs. Bellamant, I think you have left off play, which is to me surprizing, when you play'd so very well.

MRS BELLAMANT - And yet I believe, you hardly ever saw me win.

LADY CHARLOTTE - I never mind whether I win or no, if I make no Mistakes.

MR GAYWIT - Which you never fail of doing as often as you play.

LADY CHARLOTTE - Do you hear him?

EMILIA - Oh! he sets up for a Plain-dealer, that is, one who shews his Wit at the Expence of his Breeding.

LADY CHARLOTTE - Yes, and at the Expence of his Truth.

EMILIA - Never mind him, Lady Charlotte, you will have the Town on your Side.

MR GAYWIT - Yes, they will all speak for you that play against you.

LADY CHARLOTTE - This is downright insupportable.

SCENE VI

Mrs. Bellamant, Emilia, Mr. Gaywit, Lady Charlotte, Captain Bellamant.

LADY CHARLOTTE - Oh! here's Captain Bellamant shall be my Voucher.

CAPT BELLAMANT - That you may be assur'd of, Lady Charlotte, for I have so implicit a Faith in your Ladyship, that I know you are in the right before you speak.

LADY CHARLOTTE - Mr. Gaywit does not allow me to play at Quadrille.

CAPT BELLAMANT - He may as well deny that your Ladyship sees; besides, I do not lay a great deal of Weight on his Judgment, whom I never saw play at all.

LADY CHARLOTTE - Oh, abominable! then he does not live at all. I wish my whole Life was one Party at Quadrille.

CAPT BELLAMANT - As a Spaniard's is a Game at Chess, egad.

MRS BELLAMANT - I never intend to sacrifice my Time entirely to play, till I can get no one to keep me Company for nothing.

MR GAYWIT - Right, Madam, I think the Votaries to Gaming, shou'd be such as want Helps for Conversation: And none shou'd have always Cards in their Hands, but those who have nothing but the Weather in their Mouths.

MRS BELLAMANT - Thus gaming wou'd be of Service to the Publick of Wit, by taking away the Encouragers of Nonsense, as a War is of Service to a Nation, by taking the idle People out of it.

LADY CHARLOTTE - Intolerable! Mrs. Bellamant an Advocate against Play?

SCENE VII

Lord Richly, Mr. Gaywit, Captain Bellamant, Lady Charlotte, Emilia, Mrs. Bellamant.

LORD RICHLY - Who is an Advocate against Play?

LADY CHARLOTTE - Mrs. Bellamant, my Lord.

LORD RICHLY - She is grown a perfect Deserter from the Beau Monde: She has declar'd her self against Mr. Crambo too.

LADY CHARLOTTE - Against dear Mr. Crambo?

MRS BELLAMANT - I am only for indulging Reason in our Entertainments, my Lord. I must own, when I see a polite Audience pleas'd at seeing Bedlam on the Stage, I cannot forbear thinking them fit for no other Place.

LORD RICHLY - Now, I am never entertain'd better.

LADY CHARLOTTE - Nor I. Oh dear Bedlam! I have gone there once a Week for a long time. I am charm'd with those delightful Creatures, the Kings, and the Queens.

CAPT BELLAMANT - And your Ladyship has contributed abundance of Lovers, all Kings, no doubt: for he that cou'd have the Boldness to attempt you, might with much less Madness dream of a Throne.

LADY CHARLOTTE - Well, I shou'd like to be a Queen. I fancy, 'tis very pretty to be a Queen.

CAPT BELLAMANT - Were I a King, Lady Charlotte, you shou'd have your Wish.

LADY CHARLOTTE - Ay, but then, I must have you tool wou'd not have an odious filthy He–Creature for the World.

MR GAYWIT - Faith, you cannot easily find any, who is less of the He–Creature.

[Aside.

EMILIA - But, Lady Charlotte, we shall be too late for the Play.

LADY CHARLOTTE - I believe the first Act is over, so we'll go. I don't believe, I ever saw the first Act of a Play in my Life but do you think, I'll suffer you in my Coach?

MR GAYWIT - At least, you'll suffer me to put this Lady into it.

CAPT BELLAMANT - And me to put your Ladyship in.

LADY CHARLOTTE - Dear Mrs. Bellamant, your most obedient Servant.

LORD RICHLY - Shall I have the Honour, in the mean time, of entertaining you at Piquet?

MRS BELLAMANT - Your Lordship has such a vast Advantage over me

LORD RICHLY - None in the least: but if you think so, Madam, I'll give you what Points you please.

MRS BELLAMANT - For one Party then, my LordGet Cards thereYour Lordship will excuse me a Moment.

LORD RICHLY - Charming Woman!and thou art mine, as surely as I wish thee. Let me see she goes into the Country in a Fortnight. Now, if I compass my Affair in a Day or two, I shall be weary of her by that time, and her Journey will be the most agreeable thing that can happen.

SCENE VII

Mr. Modern's House.

Mrs. Modern, Mr. Bellamant.

MRS MODERN - Is it not barbarous, nay, mean, to upbraid me with what nothing but the last Necessity could have made me ask of
you?

MR BELLAMANT - You wrong me; I lament my own Necessities, not upbraid yours. My Misfortune is too publick for you not to be acquainted with it; and what restrains me from supporting the Pleasures of the best Wife in the World, may, I think, justly excuse me from supporting those of a Mistress.

MRS MODERN - Do you insult me with your Wife's Virtue? You! who have robb'd me of mine?yet Heaven will, I hope, forgive me this first Slip; and if henceforth I ever listen to the Siren Perswasions of your false ungrateful Sex, may I

MR BELLAMANT - But hear me, Madam.

MRS MODERN - Would I had never heard, nor seen, nor known you.

MR BELLAMANT - If I alone have robb'd you of your Honour, it is you alone have robb'd me of mine.

MRS MODERN - Your Honour! ridiculous! the Virtue of a Man!

MR BELLAMANT - Madam, I say, my Honour; if to rob a Woman who brought me Beauty, Fortune, Love and Virtue; if to hazard the making her miserable be no Breach of Honour, Robbers and Murderers may be honourable Men: Yet, this I have done, and this I do still for you.

MRS MODERN - We will not enter into a Detail, Mr. Bellamant, of what we have done for one another; perhaps, the Balance may be on your Side: If so, it must be still greater; for I have one Request which I must not be denied.

MR BELLAMANT - You know, if it be in my Power to grant, it is not in my Power to deny you.

MRS MODERN - Then for the sake of my Reputation, and to prevent any Jealousy in my Husband, bring me acquainted with Mrs. Bellamant.

MR BELLAMANT - Ha!

MRS MODERN - By which means we shall have more frequent Opportunities together.

MR BELLAMANT - Of what use your Acquaintance can be, I know not.

MRS MODERN - Do you scruple it? This is too plain an Evidence of your Contempt of me; you will not introduce a Woman of stain'd Virtue to your Wife: Can you, who caused my Crime, be the first to contemn me for it?

MR BELLAMANT - Since you impute my Caution to so wrong a Cause, I am willing to prove your Error.

MRS MODERN - Let our Acquaintance begin this Night then, try if you cannot bring her hither now.

MR BELLAMANT - I will try, nay, and I will succeed: for Oh! I have sacrificed the best of Wives to your Love.

MRS MODERN - I envy, not admire her for an Affection which any Woman might preserve to you.

MR BELLAMANT - I fly to execute your Commands.

MRS MODERN – Stay I

MR BELLAMANT - Speak.

MRS MODERN - I must ask one last Favour of you and yet I know not how tho' it be a Trifle, and I will repay it only to lend me another Hundred Guineas.

MR BELLAMANT - Your Request, Madam, is always a Command. I shall think Time flies with Wings of Lead till I return.

SCENE VIII

Mrs. Modern sola.

MRS MODERN - And I shall think you fly on golden Wings, my dear Gallant. Thou Ass, to think that the Heart of a Woman is to be won by Gold, as well as her Person; but thou wilt find, though a Woman often sells her Person she always gives her Heart.

SCENE IX

Mrs. Bellamant's House.

Lord Richly, Mrs. Bellamant, at Piquet.

LORD RICHLY - Six Parties successively! Sure, Fortune will change soon, or I shall believe she is not blind.

MRS BELLAMANT - No, my Lord, you either play with too great Negligence, or with such Ill−luck that I shall press my Victory no farther at present. Besides I can't help thinking five Points place the Odds on my Side.

LORD RICHLY - Can you change this Note, Madam?

MRS BELLAMANT - Let it alone, my Lord.

LORD RICHLY - Excuse me, Madam, if I am superstitiously observant to pay my Losings, before I rise from the Table, Besides, Madam, it will give me an infinite Pleasure to have the finest Woman in the World in my Debt. Do but keep it till I have the Honour of seeing you again. Nay, Madam, I must insist on it, tho' I am forced to leave it in your Hands thus

SCENE X

Mrs. Bellamant sola.

MRS BELLAMANT - What can this mean! I am confident too that he lost the last Party designedly. I observed him fix his Eyes stedfastly on mine, aud sigh, and seem careless of his GameIt must be sohe certainly hath a Design on me. I will return him this Note immediately, and am resolved never to see him more.

SCENE XI

Mr. Bellamant, Mrs. Bellamant.

MRS BELLAMANT - My Dear! where have you been all Day? I have not had one Moment of your Company since Dinner.

MR BELLAMANT - I have been upon Business of very great Consequence, my Dear.

MRS BELLAMANT - Is it fit for me to hear?

MR BELLAMANT - No, my Dear, it would only make you uneasy.

MRS BELLAMANT - Nay, then I must hear it, that I may share your Concern.

MR BELLAMANT - Indeed, it would rather aggravate it: It is not in your Power to assist me; for since you will know it, an Affair hath happen'd, which makes it necessary for me to pay an Hundred Guineas this very Evening.

MRS BELLAMANT - Is that all?

MR BELLAMANT - That indeed was once a Triflebut now it makes me uneasy.

MRS BELLAMANT - So it doth not me, because it is in my Power to supply youHere is a Note for that Sum; but I must be positively repaid within a Day or two: It is only a Friend's Money trusted in my Hands.

MR BELLAMANT - My Dear, sure when Heaven gave me thee, it gave me a Cure for every Malady of the Mind, and it hath made thee still the Instrument of all its Good to me.

MRS BELLAMANT - Be assured, I desire no greater Blessing than the continual Reflection of having pleased you.

MR BELLAMANT - Are you engaged, my Love, this Evening?

MRS BELLAMANT - Whatever Engagement I have, it is in your Power to break.

MR BELLAMANT - If you have none, I will introduce you to a new Acquaintance: One whom I believe you never visited, but must know by Sight Mrs Modern

MRS BELLAMANT - It is equal to me in what Company I am, when with you. My Eyes are so delighted with that principal Figure, that I have no Leisure to contemplate the rest of the Piece. I'll wait on you immediately.

SCENE XII

Mr. Bellamant solus.

MR BELLAMANT - What a Wretch am I! Have I either Honour or Gratitude, and can I injure such a Woman? How do I injure her! While she perceives no Abatement in my Passion, she is not injured by its inward Decay: Nor can I give her a secret Pain, while she hath no Suspicion of my secret Pleasures. Have I not found too an equal Return of Passion in my Mistress? Does she not sacrifice more for me than a Wife can? The Gallant is, indeed, indebted for the Favours he receives: But the

Husband pays dearly for what he enjoys. I hope, however, this will be the last hundred Pounds I shall be asked to lend. My Wife's having this dear Note was as lucky as it was unexpected. Ha! The same I gave this Morning to Mrs. Modern; Amazement, what can this mean?

SCENE XIII

Mr. Bellamant, Mrs. Bellamant.

MR BELLAMANT - My Dear, be not angry at my Curiosity, but pray tell me how came you by this?

MRS BELLAMANT - Pardon me, my Dear, I have a particular Reason for not telling you.

MR BELLAMANT - And I have as particular a Reason for asking it.

MRS BELLAMANT - I beg you not to press me: perhaps you will oblige me to sacrifice a Friend's Reputation.

MR BELLAMANT - The Secret shall rest in my Bosom, I assure you.

MRS BELLAMANT - But suppose, I should have promised not to suffer it from my own.

MR BELLAMANT - A Husband's Command breaks any Promise.

MRS BELLAMANT - I am surprized to see you so solicitous about a Trifle.

MR BELLAMANT - I am rather surprized to find you so tenacious of one; besides be assured, you cannot have half the Reason to suppress the Discovery, as I to insist upon it.

MRS BELLAMANT - What is your Reason?

MR BELLAMANT - The very Difficulty you make in telling it.

MRS BELLAMANT - Your Curiosity shall be satisfied then; but I beg you would defer it now. I may get absolved from my Promise of
Secrecy. I beg you would not urge me to break my Trust.

MR BELLAMANT - [Aside.]
She certainly hath not discovered my Falshood, that were impossible: besides I may satisfy my self immediately by Mrs. Modern.

MRS BELLAMANT - What makes you uneasy? I assure you, there is nothing in this worth your knowing.

MR BELLAMANT - I believe it, at least I shall give up my Curiosity to your Desire.

MRS BELLAMANT - I am ready to wait on you.

MR BELLAMANT - I must make a short Visit first on what I told you, and will call on you immediately.

SCENE XIV

Mrs. Bellamant sola.

MRS BELLAMANT -
What can have given him this Curiosity I know not, but should I have discovered the Truth, who can tell into what Suspicions it might have betrayed him? His jealous Honour might have resolved on some fatal Return to Lord Richly, had he taken it in the same way as I do; whereas by keeping the Secret, I preserve him every way from Danger; for I my self will secure his Honour without exposing his Person. I will my self give Lord Richly his Discharge. How nearly have I been unawares to the Brink of Ruin! for, surely, thelightest Suspicion of a Husband is Ruin, indeed! When Innocence can scarce our Lives defend; What Dangers must the guilty Wife attend?

ACT IV

SCENE I

SCENE, Mrs. Modern's House.

Mr. Modern, Mrs Modern

MR MODERN - In short, Madam, you shall not drive a separate Trade at my Expence. Your Person is mine, I bought it lawfully in the Church, and unless I am to profit by the Disposal, I shall keep it all for my own Use.

MRS MODERN - This Insolence is not to be borne.

MR MODERN - Have I not winked at all your Intrigues? Have I not pretended Business, to leave you and your Gallants together? Have I not been the most obsequious, observant

MRS MODERN - Out with it, you know what you are.

MR MODERN - Do you upbraid me with your Vices, Madam?

MRS MODERN - My Vicescall it Obedience to a Husband's Will. Can you deny that you have your self persuaded me to the Undertaking? Can you forget the Arguments you used to convince me that Virtue was the lightest of Bubbles?

MR MODERN - I own it all; and had I felt the Sweets of your Pleasures, as at first, I had never once upbraided you with them; but as I must more than share the Dishonour, it is surely reasonable I should share the Profit.

MRS MODERN - And have you not?

MR MODERN - What if I have

MRS MODERN - Why do you complain then?

MR MODERN - Because I find those Effects no more. Your Cards run away with the Lucre of your other Pleasures and you lose to the Knaves of your own Sex, what you get from the Fools of ours.

MRS MODERN - 'Tis false, you know I seldom lose. Nor indeed can I considerably; for I have not lately had it in my Power to stake high: Lord Richly, who was the Fountain of our Wealth, hath long been dry to me.

MR MODERN - I hope, Madam, this new Gallant will turn to a better Account.

MRS MODERN - Our Amour is yet too young to expect any Fruit from thence.

MR MODERN - As young as it is, I have Reason to believe it is grown to Perfection. Whatever Fruits I may expect from him, it is not impossible, from what hath already happened, but I may expect some from you, and that is not golden Fruit. I am sure if Women sprung from the Earth, as some Philosophers think, it was from the Clay of Egypt, not the Sands of Peru. Serpents and Crocodiles are the only Fruit they produce.

MRS MODERN - Very true, and a Wife contains the whole ten Plagues of her Country.
[Laughing.

MR MODERN - Why had I not been born a Turk, that I might have enslaved my Wife, or a Chinese, that I might have sold her!

MRS MODERN - That would have been only the Custom of the Country: You have done more, you have sold her in England; in a Country, where Women are as backward to be sold to a Lover, as to refuse him; and where Cuckold is almost the only Title of Honour that can't be bought.

MR MODERN - This ludicrous Behaviour, Madam, as ill becomes the present Subject, as the entertaining new Gallants doth the Tenderness you this Morning expressed for your Reputation. In short, it is impossible that your Amours should be secret long; and however careless you have been of me whilst I have had my Horns in my Pocket, I hope you'll take care to gild them when I am to wear them in Publick.

MRS MODERN - What would you have me do?

MR MODERN - Suffer me to discover you together; by which means we may make our Fortunes easy all at once. One good Discovery in Westminster Hall will be of greater Service than his utmost GenerosityThe Law will give you more in one Moment, than his Love for many Years.

MRS MODERN - Don't think of it.

MR MODERN - Yes, and resolve it; unless you agree to this, Madam, you must agree immediately to break up our House, and retire into the Country.

MRS MODERN - Racks and Tortures are in that Name.

MR MODERN - But many more are in that of a Prison; so you must resolve either to quit the Town, or submit to my Reasons.

MRS MODERN - When Reputation is gone, all Places are alike: when I am despised in it, I shall hate the Town as much as now I like it.

MR MODERN - There are other Places and other Towns; the whole World is the House of the Rich, and they may live in what Apartment of it they please.

MRS MODERN - I cannot resolve.

MR MODERN - But I can: if you will keep your Reputation, you shall carry it into the Country, where it will be of Service. In Town it is of noneor if it be, 'tis, like Clogs, only to those that walk on Foot; and the one will no more recommend you in an Assembly, than the other.

MRS MODERN - You never had any Love for me.

MR MODERN - Do you tax me with Want of Love for you? Have I not for your sake stood the publick Mark of Infamy? Would you have had me poorly kept you, and starv'd you?NoI could not bear to see you want, therefore have acted the Part I've done: And yet while I have wink'd at the giving up your Virtue, have I not been the most industrious to extol it every where?

MRS MODERN - So has Lord Richly, and so have all his Creatures, a common Trick among you: to blazon out the Reputation of Women, whose Virtue you have destroyed; and as industriously blacken them who have withstood you. A Deceit so stale, that your Commendation wou'd fully a Woman of Honour.

MR MODERN - I have no longer Time to reason with you; so I shall leave you to consider on what I have said.

[Exit.

MRS MODERN - What shall I do! Can I bear to be the publick Scorn of all the Malicious and Ugly of my own Sex, or to retire with a Man whom I hate and despise. Hold! there is a small Glimpse of Hope that I may avoid them both. I have reason to think Bellamant's Love as violent as he avers it. Now could I persuade him to fly away with me. Impossible! He hath still too much Tenderness for his Wife.

SCENE II

Lord Richly, Mrs Modern

LORD RICHLY - What Success, my Angel.

MRS MODERN - Hope all, my Lord, that Lovers wish or Husbands fear; she will be here.

LORD RICHLY - When?

MRS MODERN - Now, to−night, instantly.

LORD RICHLY - Thou Glory of Intrigue, what Words shall thank thee?

MRS MODERN - No Words at all, my Lord, a Hundred Pounds must witness the first Interview.

LORD RICHLY - They shall; and if she yields a Thousand.

MRS MODERN - That you must not expect yet.

LORD RICHLY - By Heaven I do, I have more Reason to expect it than you imagine; I have not been wanting to my Desires, since I left you. Fortune too seems to have watched for me. I got her to Piquet, threw away six Parties, and left her a Bank–Note of a Hundred for the Payment of Six Pound.

MRS MODERN - And did she receive it?

LORD RICHLY - With the same Reluctancy that a Lawyer or Physician would a double Fee, or a Court–Priest a Plurality.

MRS MODERN - Then there is Hope of Success, indeed.

LORD RICHLY - Hope, there is Certainty, the next Attack must carry her.

MRS MODERN - You have a hundred Friends in the Garrison, my Lord.

LORD RICHLY - And if some of them do not open the Gates for me, the Devil's in it: I have succeeded often by leaving Money in a Lady's Hands; she spends it, is unable to pay, and then I, by Virtue of my Mortgage, immediately enter upon the Premises.

MRS MODERN - You are very generous, my Lord.

LORD RICHLY - My Money shall always be the humble Servant of my Pleasures; and it is the Interest of Men of Fortune to keep up the Price of Beauty, that they may have it more among themselves.

MRS MODERN - I am as much pleased, as surprized, at this your Prospect of Success; and from this Day forward I will think with you, all Vertue to be only Pride, Caprice, and the Fear of Shame.

LORD RICHLY - Vertue, like the Ghost in Hamlet, is here, there, every where, and no where at all; its Appearance is as imaginary as that of a Ghost; and they are much the same sort of People, who are in Love with one, and afraid of the other. It is a Ghost which hath seldom haunted me, but I have had the Power of laying it.

MRS MODERN - Yes, my Lord, I am a fatal Instance of that Power.

LORD RICHLY - And the dearest, I assure you, which is some Sacrifice to your Vanity; and shortly I will make an Offering to your Revenge, the two darling Passions of your Sex.

MRS MODERN - But how is it possible for me to leave you together, without the most abrupt Rudeness?

LORD RICHLY - Never regard that; as my Success is sure, she will hereafter thank you for a Rudeness so seasonable.

MRS MODERN - Mr. Bellamant too will be with her.

LORD RICHLY - He will be as agreeably entertained with you in the next Room, and as he does not suspect the least Design in me, he will be satisfied with my being in her Company.

MRS MODERN - Sure, you will not attempt his Wife while he is in the House.

LORD RICHLY - Pish! He is in that Dependence on my Interest, that, rather than forfeit my Favour, he would be himself her Pander. I have made twenty such Men subscribe themselves Cuckolds by the Prospect of one Place, which not one of them ever had.

MRS MODERN - So that your Fools are not caught like the Fish in the Water by a Bait, but like the Dog in the Water by a Shadow.

LORD RICHLY - Besides I may possibly find a Pretence of sending him away.

MRS MODERN - Go then to the Chocolate–House, and leave a Servant to bring you word of their Arrival. It will be better you should come in to them than they find you here.

LORD RICHLY - I will be guided by you in all things, and be assured the Consummation of my Wishes shall be the Success of your own.

[Exit Lord Richly.

MRS MODERN - That they shall, indeed, tho' in a way you little imagine: This Forwardness of Mrs. Bellamant's meets my swiftest Wishes: Could I once give Bellamant Reason to suspect his Wife, I despair not of the happiest Effect of his Passion for meHa! he's here and alone.

SCENE III

Mr. Bellamant, Mrs Modern

MRS MODERN - here's Mrs. Bellamant?

MR BELLAMANT - She will be here immediately: But I chose a few Moments Privacy with you, first to deliver you this, and next to ask you one Question, which do not be startled at. Pray, how did you employ that Note you received this Morning?

MRS MODERN - Nay, if you expect an Account of me, perhaps you will still do so; so let me return you this.

MR BELLAMANT - Do not so injuriously mistake me. Nothing but the most extraordinary Reason could force me to ask you; know then that the very Note you had of me this Morning, I received within this Hour from my Wife.

MRS MODERN - Ha! ha! ha!

MR BELLAMANT - Why do you laugh, Madam?

MRS MODERN - Out of Triumph, to see what empty Politicians Men are found, when they oppose their weak Heads to ours! On my Conscience, a Parliament of Women would be of very great Service to the Nation.

MR BELLAMANT - Were all Ladies capable as Mrs. Modern, I should be very ready to vote on their Side.

MRS MODERN - Nay, nay, Sir, you must not leave out your Wife, especially you that have the best Wife in the World, ha, ha, ha.

MR BELLAMANT - Forgive me, Madam, if I have been too partial to a Woman, whose whole Business hath been to please me.

MRS MODERN - Oh! You have no Reason to be ashamed of your good Opinion; you are not singular in it, I assure you; Mrs Bellamant will have more Votes than one.

MR BELLAMANT - I am indifferent how many she has, since I am sure she will make Interest but for one.

MRS MODERN - "It is the Curse of Fools to be secure, And that be thine and Altamont's, ha, ha, ha.

MR BELLAMANT - I cannot guess your Meaning.

MRS MODERN - Then to introduce my Explanation, the Note you lent me, I lost at Piquet to Lord Richly.

MR BELLAMANT - To Lord Richly!

MRS MODERN - Who perhaps might dispose of it to some who might lend it to others, who might give it to those who might lose it to your Wife.

MR BELLAMANT - I know not what to suppose.

MRS MODERN - Nor I; for sure one cannot suppose, especially since you have the best Wife in the World; one cannot suppose, that it could be a Present from Lord Richly to her self, that she received it, that in Return she hath sent him an Assignation to meet her here.

MR BELLAMANT - Suppose! Hell and Damnation, No.

MRS MODERN - But certainly, one could not affirm that this is Truth.

MR BELLAMANT - Affirm!

MRS MODERN - And yet all this is true, as true as she is false. Nay, you shall have an Instance! an immediate undeniable Instance. You shall see it with your own Eyes, and hear it with your own Ears.

MR BELLAMANT - Am I alive?

MRS MODERN - If all the Husbands of these best Wives in the World are dead, we are a strange Nation of Ghosts. If you will be prudent, and be like the rest of your Brethren, keep the Affair secret, I assure you I'll never discover it.

MR BELLAMANT - Secret! Yes, as inward Fire, till sure Destruction shall attend its Blaze. But why do I rage? it is impossible; she must be innocent.

MRS MODERN - Then Lord Richly is still a greater Villain to belye that Innocence to me: But give your self no Pain of Anxiety since you are so shortly to be certain. Go fetch her hither, Lord Richly will be here almost as soon as you; then feign some Excuse to leave the Room, I will soon follow you, and convey you where you shall have an Opportunity of being a Witness either to her Innocence or her Guilt.

MR BELLAMANT - This Goodness, my sweetest Creature, shall bind me yours for ever.

MRS MODERN - To convince you That is all I desire, I am willing to leave the Town and Reputation at once, and retire with you wherever you please.

MR BELLAMANT - That must be the Subject of our future Thoughts. I can think of nothing now but Satisfaction in this Affair.

[Exit.

MRS MODERN - Do you demur to my Offer, Sir! Oh, the Villain! I find, I am to be only a momentary Object of his looser Pleasures, and his Wife yet sits nearest his Heart. But I shall change the Angel Form she wears into a Devil's. Nor shall my Revenge stop thereBut at present I must resolve my Temper into a Calm Latley

SCENE IV

Mrs. Modern, Lately

MRS MODERN - Come hither, Lately, get me some Citron–Water. I am horribly out of Order.

LATELY - Yes, Madam.

MRS MODERN - To be slighted in this manner: Insupportable! What is the Fool doing.

LATELY - There is no Citron–Water left. Your Ladyship drank the last half Pint this Morning.

MRS MODERN - Then bring the Cinnamon–Water, or the Surfeit–Water, or the Aniseed–Water, or the Plague–Water, or any Water.

LATELY - Here, Madam.

[Brings the Bottle and Glass, and fills.

MRS MODERN - [Drinks. Looks in the Glass.]
Lord, how I look. Oh! Frightful I am quite shocking.

LATELY - In my Opinion your Ladyship never looked better.

MRS MODERN - Go, you Flatterer; I look like my Lady Grim.

LATELY - Where are your Ladyship's little Eyes, your short Nose, your wan Complexion, and your low Forehead?

MRS MODERN - Which Nature, in order to hide, hath carefully placed between her Shoulders; so that if you view her behind, she seems to walk without her Head, and lessen the Miracle of St. Dennis.

LATELY - Then her left Hip is tucked up under her Arm, like the Hilt of a Beau's Sword; and her disdainful Right is never seen, like its Blade.

MRS MODERN - Then she has two Legs, one of which seems to be the Dwarf of the other, and are alike in nothing but their Crookedness.

LATELY - And yet she thinks herself a Beauty.

MRS MODERN - She is, indeed, the Perfection of Ugliness.

LATELY - And a Wit I warrant you.

MRS MODERN - No doubt she must be very quick–sighted, for her Eyes are almost crept into her Brain.

LATELY – Mrs Modern. He, he, he.

MRS MODERN - And yet the detestable Creature hath not had Sense enough, with all her Deformity to preserve her Reputation.

LATELY - I never heard, I own, any thing against that.

MRS MODERN - You hear, you Fool, you Dunce, what should you hear? Have not all the Town heard of a certain Colonel?

LATELY - Oh! Lud! What a Memory I have! Oh! yes, Madam, she has been quite notorious. It is surprizing, a little Discretion should not preserve her from such publick

MRS MODERN - If she had my Discretion, or yours, Lately

LATELY - Your Ladyship will make me proud, indeed, Madam.

MRS MODERN - I never could see any want of Sense in you, Lately I could not bear to have an insensible Creature about me. I know several Women of Fashion I could not support for a tiring Woman. What think you of Mrs. Charmer?

LATELY - Think of her! that were I a Man, she shou'd be the last Woman I attacked. I think her an ugly, ungenteel, squinting, flirting, impudent, odious, dirty Puss.

MRS MODERN - Upon my Word, Lately, you have a vast deal of Wit too.

LATELY - I am beholden for all my Wit, as well as my Clothes, to your Ladyship. I wish, your Ladyship wore out as much Clothes as you do Wit; I should soon grow rich.

MRS MODERN - You shall not complain of either. Oh! [Knocking.] They are come, and I will receive them in another Room.

[Exit.

LATELY - I know not whether my Talent of Praise, or of Slander, is of more Service to me; whether I get more by flattering my Lady, or abusing all her Acquaintance.

SCENE V

John, Lately

JOHN - So, Mrs. Lately, you forget your old Acquaintance; but Times are coming when I may be as good as another, and you may repent your Inconstancy.

LATELY - Odious Fellow!

JOHN - I would have you to know, I look on my self to be as good as your new Sweetheart, tho' he has more Lace on his Livery, and may be a Year or two younger, and as good a Man I am too; and so you may tell him. Why does not he stay at Home? What does he come into our Family for?

LATELY - Who gave you Authority to enquire, Sirrah?

JOHN -
Marry, that did you, when you gave me a Promise to marry me; well, I shall say no more; but Times are a coming,
when you may wish you had not forsaken me. I have a Secret.

LATELY - A Secret! Oh, let me hear it.

JOHN - No, no, Mistress, I shall keep my Secrets as well as you can yours.

LATELY - Nay, now you are unkind; you know, tho' I suffer Tom Brisk to visit me, you have my Heart still.

JOHN - Ah! you do but say so! you know too well how much I love you. Then I'll tell you, my Dear, I am going to the Devil for you.

LATELY - The Devil, you are. Going to the Devil for me! what does the Fool mean?

JOHN - Ay, I am to get a hundred Pounds that you may marry me.

LATELY - A hundred Pounds! and how are you to get a hundred Pounds, my dear John?

JOHN - Only by a little Swearing.

LATELY - What are you to swear?

JOHN - Nay, if I tell you, it would be double Perjury; for I have sworn already, I would not trust it with any Body.

LATELY - Oh! but you may trust me.

JOHN - And if you should trust some Body else.

LATELY - The Devil fetch me, if I do.

JOHN - Then my Master is to give me an hundred Pound to swear that he is a Cuckold.

LATELY - What's this?

JOHN - Why, my Master has offered me an hundred Pound, if I discover my Lady and Mr. Bellamant in a proper Manner; and let me but see them together, I'll swear to the Manner, I warrant you.

LATELY - But can you do this with a safe Conscience?

JOHN - Conscience, pshaw; which would you choose, a Husband with a hundred Pound, or a safe Conscience? Come give me a Dram out of your Mistress's Closet; and there I'll tell you more.

LATELY - Come along with me.

SCENE VI

SCENE changes to another Apartment.

Lord Richly, Mr. Bellamant, Mrs. Bellamant, Mrs Modern

LORD RICHLY - Well, Madam, you have drawn a most delightful Sketch of Life.

MRS MODERN - Then it is still Life; for I dare swear there never were such People breathing.

MRS BELLAMANT - Don't you believe then, Madam, it is possible for a married Couple to be happy in one another, without desiring any other Company?

MRS MODERN - Indeed, I do not know what it may have been in the Plains of Arcadia; but truly, in those of Great Britain, I believe not.

LORD RICHLY - I must subscribe to that too.

MRS BELLAMANT - Mr. Bellamant, what say you?

MR BELLAMANT - Oh! my Dear, I am entirely of your Mind.

LORD RICHLY - This is a Miracle almost equal to the other, to see a Husband and Wife of the same Opinion. I must be a Convert too; for it would be the greatest Miracle of all to find Mrs. Bellamant in the wrong.

MRS BELLAMANT - It would be a much greater to find want of Complaisance in Lord Richly.

MR BELLAMANT - [Aside.]
Confusion!

MRS MODERN - Nay, Madam, this is hardly so; for I have heard his Lordship say the same in your Absence.

LORD RICHLY - Dear Bellamant, I believe, I have had an Opportunity to serve you this Afternoon. I have spoke to Lord Powerful, he says, he is very willing to do for you. Sir Peter, they tell me, is given over, and I fancy, you may find my Lord at Home now.

MR BELLAMANT - I shall take another Opportunity, my Lord, a particular Affair now preventing me.

LORD RICHLY - The Loss of an Hour hath been often the Loss of a Place; and unless you have something of greater Consequence,
I must advise you as a Friend.

MR BELLAMANT - I shall find a Method of thanking you.

[Aside.

MRS MODERN - Make this a Handle to slip out, I'll come into the next Room to you.

[Aside to Mr. Bellamant.

MR BELLAMANT - My Lord, I am very much obliged to your Friendship. My Dear, I'll call on you in my Return: Mrs. Modern, I am your humble Servant.

SCENE VII

Lord Richly, Mrs. Bellamant, Mrs Modern

LORD RICHLY - I wish you Success, you may command any thing in my Power to forward it.

MRS BELLAMANT - Mr. Bellamant is more indebted to your Lordship, than he will be ever able to pay.

LORD RICHLY - Mr. Bellamant, Madam, has a Friend, who is able to pay more Obligations than I can lay on him.

MRS MODERN - I am forc'd to be guilty of a great piece of Rudeness, by leaving you one Moment.

LORD RICHLY - And I shall not be guilty of losing it.

[Aside.

MRS BELLAMANT - What can this mean?

[Aside.

SCENE VIII

Lord Richly, Mrs. Bellamant.

LORD RICHLY - And can you, Madam, think of retiring from the general Admiration of Mankind?

MRS BELLAMANT - With Pleasure, my Lord, to the particular Admiration of him who is to me all Mankind.

LORD RICHLY - Is it possible any Man can be so happy?

MRS BELLAMANT - I hope, my Lord, you think Mr. Bellamant so.

LORD RICHLY - If he be, I pity him much less for his Losses, than I envy him the Love of her in whose Power it may be to redress them.

MRS BELLAMANT - You surprize me, my Lord: In my Power!

LORD RICHLY - Yes, Madam; for whatever is in the Power of Man, is in yours: I am sure, what little Assistance mine can give, is readily at your Devotion. My Interest and Fortune are all in these dear Hands; in short, Madam, I have languish'd a long Time for an Opportunity to tell you, that I have the most violent Passion for you.

MRS BELLAMANT - My Lord, I have been unwilling to understand you; but now your Expression leaves me no other Doubt, but whether I hate or despise you most.

LORD RICHLY - Are these the ungrateful Returns you give my Love?

MRS BELLAMANT - Is this the Friendship you have profess'd to Mr. Bellamant?

LORD RICHLY - I'll make his Fortune. Let this be an Instance of my future Favours.

[Puts a Bank–Note in her Hand; she throws it away.

MRS BELLAMANT - And this of my Reception of them. Be assur'd, my Lord, if you ever renew this unmannerly Attack on my Honour, I will be reveng'd; my Husband shall know his Obligations to you.

LORD RICHLY - I have gone too far to retreat, Madam; if I cannot be the Object of your Love, let me be oblig'd to your Prudence. How many Families are supported by this Method which you start at? Does not many a Woman in this Town drive her Husband's Coach?

MRS BELLAMANT - My Lord, this Insolence is intolerable, and from this Hour I never will see your Face again.

[A Noise without.

LORD RICHLY - Hey! what is the meaning of this?

Mr. Modern with Servants, Mr. Bellamant, Mrs. Modern, Lord Richly, Mrs. Bellamant.

MR MODERN - Come out, Strumpet, show thy Face and thy Adulterer's before the World; thou shalt be a severe Example of the Vengeance of an injur'd Husband.

LORD RICHLY - I have no farther Business here at present; for I fear, more Husbands have discover'd Injuries, than one.

[Exit.

MRS BELLAMANT - Protect me, Heavens! what do I see!

MR BELLAMANT - This was a Master-piece of my evil Genius.

MRS MODERN - Sir, this Insult upon my Reputation shall not go unreveng'd; I have Relations, Brothers, who will defend their Sister's Fame from the base Attacks of a perfidious Husband, from any Shame he would bring on her Innocence.

MR MODERN - Thou hast a Forehead that would defend it self from any Shame whatsoever; that you have grafted on my Forehead, I thank you, and this worthy Gentleman.

MRS MODERN - Sir, you shall smart for the Falsehood of this Accusation.

[Exit.

MR MODERN - Madam, you shall smart for the Truth of it; this honest Man, [Pointing to the Servant.] is Evidence of the Fact, of your Dishonour and mine. And for you, Sir, [To Bellamant.] you may depend upon it, I shall take the strictest Satisfaction which the Law will give me: so I shall leave you at present, to give Satisfaction to your Wife.

[Exeunt.

Mr. Bellamant, Mrs. Bellamant.

MR BELLAMANT - [After some Pause.]
When the Criminal turns his own Accuser, the merciful Judge becomes his Advocate: Guilt is too plainly written in my Face to admit of a Denial, and I stand prepar'd to receive what Sentence you please.

MRS BELLAMANT - As you are your own Accuser, be your own Judge; you can inflict no Punishment on your self equal to what I feel.

MR BELLAMANT - Death has no Terrors equal to that Thought. Ha! I have involv'd thee too in my Ruin, and thou must be the wretched Partaker of my Misfortunes.

MRS BELLAMANT - While I was assur'd of your Truth, I could have thought that Happiness enough: yet, I have still this to comfort me, the same Moment that has betray'd your Guilt, has discover'd my Innocence.

MR BELLAMANT - Oh! thou ungrateful Fool, what Stores of Bliss hast thou in one vicious Moment destroy'd! [To himself.] Oh! My Angel, how have I requited all your Love and Goodness? For what have I forsaken thy tender virtuous Passion?

MRS BELLAMANT - For a new one. How could I be so easily deceiv'd? How could I imagine there was such Truth in Man, in that inconstant fickle Sex, who are so prone to Change; that to indulge their Fondness for Variety, they would grow weary of a Paradise to wander in a Desert?

MR BELLAMANT - How weak is that Comparison to shew the Difference between thee, and every other Woman!

MRS BELLAMANT - I once had that Esteem of you; but hereafter, I shall think all Men the same; and when I have wean'd my self of my Love for you, will hate them all alike.

MR BELLAMANT - Thy Sentence is too just. I own, I have deserv'd it, I never merited so good a Wife. Heaven saw it had given too much, and thus has taken the Blessing from me.

MRS BELLAMANT - You will soon think otherwise. If Absence from me can bring you to those Thoughts, I am resolv'd to favour them.

MR BELLAMANT - Thou shalt enjoy thy Wish, we will part, part this Night, this Hour. Yet, let me ask one Favour, the Ring which was a Witness of our Meeting, let it be so of our Separation. Let me bear this as a Memorial of our Love. This shall remind me of all the tender Moments we have had together, and serve to aggravate my Sorrows: Henceforth, I'll study only to be miserable; let Heaven make you happy, and curse me as it pleases.

MRS BELLAMANT - It cannot make me more wretched than you have made me.

MR BELLAMANT - Yet, do believe me when I swear, I never injur'd you with any other Woman. Nay, believe me when I swear how much soever I may have deserv'd the Shame I suffer, I did not now deserve it.

MRS BELLAMANT - And, must we part?

MR BELLAMANT - Since it obliges you.

MRS BELLAMANT - That I may have nothing to remember you by, take back this, and this, and this, and all the thousand Embraces thou hast given metill I die in thy loved Armsand thus we part for ever.

MR BELLAMANT - Ha!

MRS BELLAMANT - Oh! I forgive thee all: forget it as a frightful Dreamit was no more, and I awake to real Joy.

MR BELLAMANT - Oh! let me press thee to my Heart; for every Moment that I hold thee thus, gives Bliss beyond Expression, a Bliss no Vice can give. Now Life appears desirable again. Yet shall I not see thee miserable? Shall I not see my Children suffer for their Father's Crime?

MRS BELLAMANT - Indulge no more uneasy Thoughts; Fortune may have Blessings yet in store for us and them.

MR BELLAMANT - Excellent Goodness! my future Days shall have no Wish, no Labour, but for thy Happiness; and from this Hour, I'll never give thee Cause of a Complaint. And whatsoever Rocks our Fates may lay In Life's hard Passage to obstruct our way; Patient, the toilsome Journey I'll abide; And bless my Fortune with so dear a Guide.

ACT V

SCENE I

SCENE Mr. Bellamant's House

Emilia speaking to a Servant, afterwards Lady Charlotte.

EMILIA - It is very strange you will not give me the Liberty of denying myself; that you will force me to be at Home, whether I will or no.

SERVANT - I had no such Order from your Ladyship.

EMILIA - Well, well, go wait upon her up. I am but in an ill Humour to receive such a Visit; I must try to make it as short as I can.

LADY CHARLOTTE - Emilia, Good–morrow: Am not I an early Creature? I have been so frightned with some News I have heard I am heartily concern'd for you, my Dear, I hope the Fright has not done you any Mischief.

EMILIA - I am infinitely oblig'd to you, Lady Charlotte.

LADY CHARLOTTE - Oh! I could not stay one Moment; you see, I hurried into my Chair to you half undrest; never was Creature in such a Pickle, so frightful; Lud! I was oblig'd to draw all the Curtains round me.

EMILIA - I don't perceive you had any Reason for that, Lady Charlotte .

LADY CHARLOTTE - Why, did you ever see any thing so hideous, so odious as this Gown? Well, Emilia, you certainly have the prettiest Fancy in the World. I like what you have on now, better than Lady Pinup's , tho' hers cost so much more. Some People have the strangest way of laying out their Money. You remember our Engagement to–night.

EMILIA - You must excuse me; it will look very odd to see me abroad on this Occasion.

LADY CHARLOTTE - Not odd in the least. No Body minds these Things. There's no Rule upon such Occasions. Sure, you don't intend to stay at Home, and receive formal Visits.

EMILIA - No; but I intend to stay at Home, and receive no Visits.

LADY CHARLOTTE - Why, Child, you will be laugh'd at by all the Town. There never was such a Thing done in the World; staying at Home is quite left off upon all Occasions; a Woman scarce stays at Home a Week for the Death of a Husband. Dear Emilia, don't be so aukward: I can make no Excuse for you; Lady Polite will never forgive you.

EMILIA - That I shall be sorry for: but I had rather not be forgiven by her, than by my self.

SCENE II

Captain Bellamant, Lady Charlotte, Emilia

CAPT BELLAMANT - Sister, Good-morrow; Lady Charlotte abroad so early!

LADY CHARLOTTE - You may well be surpriz'd; I have not been out at this Hour, these fifty Years.

CAPT BELLAMANT - You will never be able to hold it out till Night.

EMILIA - [Aside.]
I am sure if she should take it in her Head to stay with me, I shall not: And unless some dear Creature, like herself, should come and take her away, I seem to be in Danger.

LADY CHARLOTTE - [To Bellamant after a Whisper.]
Don't tell me of what I said last Night. Last Night was last Year; an Age ago: and I have the worst Memory in the World.

CAPT BELLAMANT - You seem to want one, egad!

LADY CHARLOTTE - Indeed, I do not. A Memory would be of no Use to me; for I was never of the same Mind twice in my Life: and tho' I should remember what I said at one Time, I should as certainly remember not to do it at another.

CAPT BELLAMANT - You dear agreeable Creature! Sure, never two People were so like one another as you and I are. We think alike, we act alike, and some People think, we are very much alike in the Face.

LADY CHARLOTTE - Do you hear him, Emilia? He has made one of the most shocking Compliments to me; I believe, I shall never be able to bear a Looking-glass again.

CAPT BELLAMANT - Faith, and if it was not for the Help of a Looking-glass, you would be the most unhappy Creature in the World.

LADY CHARLOTTE - Impertinent!

CAPT BELLAMANT - For then you would be the only Person debarr'd from seeing the finest Face in the World.

EMILIA - Very fine, indeed.

LADY CHARLOTTE - Civil enough. I think, I begin to endure the Wretch again now.

CAPT BELLAMANT - Keep but in that Mind half an Hour

LADY CHARLOTTE - Emilia, Good–morrow, you will excuse the Shortness of my Visit.

EMILIA - No Apologies on that Account, Lady Charlotte.

LADY CHARLOTTE - You are a good Creature, and know the continual Hurry of Business I am in. Don't you follow me, you Thing, you!

[To Capt Bellamant.

CAPT BELLAMANT - Indeed, Lady Charlotte, but I shall, and I hope to some Purpose.

[Aside.

SCENE III

Emilia alone.

EMILIA - So, I am once more left to my own Thoughts. Heaven knows, they are like to afford me little Entertainment. Oh! Gaywit! too much I sympathize with thy Uneasiness. Didst thou know the Pangs I feel on thy Account, thy generous Heart would suffer more on mine. Ha! my Words have rais'd a Spirit.

SCENE IV

Emilia, Mr Gaywit

MR GAYWIT - I hope, Madam, you will excuse a Visit at so unseasonable an Hour.

EMILIA - Had you come a little earlier, you had met a Mistress here.

MR GAYWIT - I met the Lady you mean, Madam, at the Door, and Captain Bellamant with her.

EMILIA - You are the most Cavalier Lover I know, you are no more jealous of a Rival with your Mistress, than the most polite Husband is of one with his Wife.

MR GAYWIT - A Man should not be jealous of his Friend, Madam, and I believe, Captain Bellamant will be such to me in the highest Manner. I wish, I were so blest in another Heart, as he appears to be in Lady Charlotte's. I wish, I were as certain of gaining the Woman I do love, as of losing her I do not.

EMILIA - I suppose, if your Amour be of any Date, you can easily guess at the Impressions you have made.

MR GAYWIT - No, nor can she guess at the Impression she has made on me; for unless my Eyes have done it, I never acquainted her with my Passion.

EMILIA - And that your Eyes have done it, you may be assur'd, if you have seen her often. The Love that can be conceal'd, must be very cold indeed; but, methinks, it is something particular in you to desire to conceal it.

MR GAYWIT - I have been always fearful to disclose a Passion, which I know not whether it be in my Power to pursue. I would not even have given her the Uneasiness to pity me, much less have tried to raise her Love.

EMILIA - If you are so tender of her, take care you never let her suspect so much Generosity. That may give her a secret Pang.

MR GAYWIT - Heaven forbid it should, one equal to those I feel; lest, while I am endeavouring to make my Addresses practicable, she should unadvisedly receive those of another.

EMILIA - If she can discover your Love as plain as I can, I think you may be easy on that Account.

MR GAYWIT - He must dote like me who can conceive the Ecstasy these Words have given.

EMILIA - [Knocking.]
Come in.

SERVANY - Your Honour's Servant, Sir, is below.

MR GAYWIT - I come to himMadam, your most obedient Servant; I go on Business which will by Noon give me the Satisfaction of thinking I have preserv'd the best of Fathers to the best of Women.

EMILIA - I know, he means mine; but why do I mention that, when every Action of his Life leaves me no other Doubt than whether it convinces me more of his Love, or of his deserving mine.

SCENE V

Lord Richly's House.

Lord Richly, Servant.

LORD RICHLY - Desire Mr. Bellamant to walk in. What can the Meaning of this Visit be? Perhaps, he comes to make me Proposals concerning his Wife; but my Love shall not get so far the better of my Reason, as to lead me to an extravagant Price; I'll not go above two Thousand, that's positive.

Lord Richly, Mr. Bellamant.

LORD RICHLY - My dear Bellamant.

MR BELLAMANT - My Lord, I have receiv'd an Obligation from you, which I thus return.

[Gives him a Bank–Bill.

LORD RICHLY - Pshaw! Trifles of this Nature can hardly be call'd Obligations; I would do twenty times as much for dear Jack Bellamant.

MR BELLAMANT - The Obligation indeed was to my Wife, nor hath she made you a small Return; since it is to her Intreaty you owe your present Safety, your Life.

LORD RICHLY -
I am not appriz'd of the Danger; but would owe my Safety to no one, sooner than to Mrs. Bellamant.

MR BELLAMANT -
Come, come, my Lord; this Prevarication is low and mean: You know, you have us'd me basely, villanously; and
under the Cover of Acquaintance and Friendship have attempted to corrupt my Wife; for which, but that I would
not suffer the least Breath of Scandal to sully her Reputation, I would exact such Vengeance on thee

LORD RICHLY - Sir, I must acquaint you, that this is a Language I have not been us'd to.

MR BELLAMANT - No, the Language of Flatterers and hireling Sycophants has been what you have dealt inWretches, whose Honour and Love are as venal as their Praise. Such your Title might awe, or your Fortune bribe to Silence; such you should have dealt with, and not have dared to injure a Man of Honour.

LORD RICHLY - This is such Presumption

MR BELLAMANT - No, my Lord, yours was the Presumption, mine is only Justice, nay, and mild too; unequal to your Crime which requires a Punishment from my Hand, not from my Tongue.

LORD RICHLY - Do you consider who I am?

MR BELLAMANT - Were you as high as Heraldy could lift you, you should not injure me unpunish'd. Where Grandeur can give Licence to Oppression, the People must be Slaves, let them boast what Liberty they please.

LORD RICHLY - Sir, you shall hear of this.

MR BELLAMANT - I shall be ready to justify my Words by any Action you dare provoke me to: And be assur'd of this, if ever I discover any future Attempts of yours to my Dishonour, your Life shall be its Sacrifice. Hence forward, my Lord, let us behave, as if we had never known one another.

[Exit.

LORD RICHLY - Here's your Man of Sense now,He was half ruin'd in the House of Lords a few Days ago, and is in a fair Way of going the other Step in Westminster–Hall in a few Days more; yet, has the Impudence to threaten a Man of my Fortune and Quality, for attempting to debauch his Wife; which many a Fool, who rides in his Coach and Six, would have had Sense enough to have wink'd at.

SCENE VII

Lord Richly, Mr Gaywit

MR GAYWIT - Your Lordship is contemplative.

LORD RICHLY - So, Nephew, by this early Visit, I suppose you had ill Luck last Night; for where Fortune frowns on you, she always smiles on me, by blessing me with your Company.

MR GAYWIT - I have long since put it out of the Power of Fortune to do me either Favour or Injury. My Happiness is now in the Power of another Mistress.

LORD RICHLY - And thou art too pretty a Fellow not to have that Mistress in your Power.

MR GAYWIT - The Possession of her, and in her of all my Desires, depends on your Consent.

LORD RICHLY - You know, Harry, you have my Consent to possess all the Women in Town, except those few that I am particular with: Provided you fall not foul on mine, you may board and plunder what Vessels you please.

MR GAYWIT - This is a Vessel, my Lord, neither to be taken by force, nor hired by Gold. I must buy her for Life, or not board at all.

LORD RICHLY - Then the principal thing to be consider'd, is her Cargo. To marry a Woman meerly for her Person, is buying an empty Vessel: And a Woman is a Vessel, which a Man will grow cursed weary of in a long Voyage.

MR GAYWIT - My Lord, I have had some Experience in Women, and I believe, that I never could be weary of the Woman I now love.

LORD RICHLY - Let me tell you, I have had some Experience too, and I have been weary of forty Women that I have lov'd.

MR GAYWIT - And, perhaps, in all that Variety, you may not have found one of equal Excellence with her I mean.

LORD RICHLY - And pray, who is this Paragon you mean?

MR GAYWIT - Must I, my Lord, when I have painted the finest Woman in the World, be oblig'd to write Miss Bellamant's Name to the Picture?

LORD RICHLY - Miss Bellamant!

MR GAYWIT - Yes, Miss Bellamant.

LORD RICHLY - You know Mr. Bellamant's Losses; you know what happen'd Yesterday, which may entirely finish his Ruin; and the Consequence of his Ruin must be the Ruin of his Daughter; Which will certainly throw her Vertue into your Power; for Poverty as surely brings a Woman to Capitulation, as Scarcity of Provisions does a Garrison.

MR GAYWIT - I cannot take this Advice, my Lord: I would not take Advantage from the Misfortunes of any; but surely, not of the Woman I love.

LORD RICHLY - Well, Sir, you shall ask me no more; for if my Consent to your Ruin will oblige you, you have it.

MR GAYWIT - My Lord, I shall ever remember this Goodness, and will be ready to sign any Instrument to secure a very large Fortune to Lady Charlotte when you please.

SCENE VIII

Lord Richly solus.

LORD RICHLY - Now if he takes my Consent from my own Word, I may deny it afterwards, so I gain the whole Estate for my Daughter, and bring an entire Destruction upon Bellamant and his whole Family: Charming Thought! that would be a Revenge, indeed; nay, it may accomplish all my Wishes too; Mrs. Bellamant may be mine at last.

SCENE IX

Lord Richly, Mr Modern

MR MODERN - My Lord, I was honour'd with your Commands.

LORD RICHLY - I believe, I shall procure the Place for you, Sir.

MR MODERN - My Obligations to your Lordship are so infinite, that I must always be your Slave.

LORD RICHLY - I am concern'd for your Misfortune, Mr Modern

MR MODERN - It is a common Misfortune, my Lord, to have a bad Wife. I am something happier than my Brethren in the Discovery.

LORD RICHLY - That, indeed, may make you amends more ways than one. I cannot dissuade you from the most rigorous Prosecution; for, tho' dear Jack Bellamant be my particular Friend, yet in

Cases of this nature, even Friendship it self must be thrown up. Injuries of this kind are not to be forgiven.

MR MODERN - Very true, my Lord; he has robb'd me of the Affections of a Wife, whom I have lov'd as tenderly as my self: Forgive my Tears, my LordI have lost all I held dear in this World.

LORD RICHLY - I pity you, indeed; but comfort your self with the Hopes of Revenge.

MR MODERN - Alas! my Lord, what Revenge can equal the Dishonour he has brought upon my Family? Think on that, my Lord; on the Dishonour I must endure. I cannot name the Title they will give me.

LORD RICHLY - It is shocking, indeed!

MR MODERN - My Ease for ever lost, my Quiet gone, my Honour stain'd, my Honour, my Lord. Oh! 'tis a tender Wound.

LORD RICHLY - Laws cannot be too rigorous against Offences of this Nature: Juries cannot give too great Damages. To attempt the Wife of a FriendTo what Wickedness will Men arrive?Mr. Modern, I own, I cannot blame you in pushing your Revenge to the utmost Extremity.

MR MODERN - That I am resolv'd on. I have just receiv'd an Appointment from your Lordship's Nephew, Mr. Gaywit; I suppose to give me some Advice in the Affair.

LORD RICHLY - [Aside.]
Ha! that must be to dissuade him from the ProsecutionMr. Modern, if you please, I'll set you down, I have some particular Business with him: besides, if he knows any thing that can be of Service to you, my Commands shall enforce the Discovery. Bid the Coachman pull up.

MR MODERN - I am the most oblig'd of all your Lordship's Slaves.

SCENE X

Another Apartment.

Lady Charlotte, Captain Bellamant and Servant.

LADY CHARLOTTE - My Lord gone out! then d'ye hear! I am at home to no Body.

CAPT BELLAMANT - That's kind, indeed, Lady Charlotte, to let me have you all to my self.

LADY CHARLOTTE - You! you confident thing! how came you here? don't you remember, I bad you not to follow me?

CAPT BELLAMANT - Yes, but it's so long ago, that I'm surpriz'd you should remember it.

LADY CHARLOTTE - Indeed, Sir, I always remember to avoid what I don't like. I suppose you don't know that I hate you of all things.

CAPT BELLAMANT - Not I, upon my Soul! the Duce take me, if I did not think, you had lik'd me, as well as I lik'd you, ha, ha.

LADY CHARLOTTE - I like you, impossible! why don't you know, that you are very ugly?

CAPT BELLAMANT - Pshaw! that's nothing; that will all go off; a Month's Marriage takes off the Homeliness of a Husband's Face, as much as it does the Beauty of a Wife's.

LADY CHARLOTTE - And so you would insinuate that I might be your Wife? O horrible! shocking Thought!

CAPT BELLAMANT - Nay, Madam, I am as much frighten'd at the Thoughts of Marriage, as you can be.

LADY CHARLOTTE - Indeed, Sir, you need not be under any Apprehensions of that kind, upon my Account.

CAPT BELLAMANT - Indeed, but I am, Madam; for what an unconsolable Creature wou'd you be, if I shou'd take it in my Head to marry any other Woman.

LADY CHARLOTTE - Well, he has such an excessive Assurance that I am not really sure, whether he is not agreeable. Let me die, if I am not under some sort of Suspense about it and yet I am n't neitherfor to be sure I don't like the thing and yet methinks, I do too and yet I do not know what I should do with him neither. Hi! hi! hi! this is the foolishest Circumstance that ever I knew in my Life.

CAPT BELLAMANT - Very well! sure, Marriage begins to run in your Head at last; Madam.

LADY CHARLOTTE - A propos! do you know that t'other Day, Lady Betty Shuttlecock and I laid down the prettiest Scheme of Matrimony, that ever enter'd into the Taste of People of Condition.

CAPT BELLAMANT - O! pray let's hear it.

LADY CHARLOTTE - In the first place then, when ever she or I marry, I am resolv'd positively to be Mistress of my self; I must have my House to my self, my Coach to my self, my Servants to my self, my Table, Time, and Company to my self; Nay, and sometimes when I have a mind to be out of Humour, my Bed to my self.

CAPT BELLAMANT - Right, Madam, for a Wife and a Husband always together, are, to be sure, the flattest Company in the World.

LADY CHARLOTTE - O detestable! then I will be sure to have my own Humour in ev'ry thing; to go, come, dine, dance, play, sup, at all Hours, and in whatever Company I have a mind to; and if ever he pretends to put on a grave Face, upon my enjoying any one of those Articles, I am to burst out in his Face a laughing. Won't that be prodigious pleasant? ha! ha! ha!

CAPT BELLAMANT - O charmingly charming! ha, ha, what a contemptible Creature is a Woman, that never does any thing, without consulting her Husband?

LADY CHARLOTTE - Nay, there you're mistaken again, Sir: For I would never do any thing without consulting my Husband.

CAPT BELLAMANT - How so, dear Madam?

LADY CHARLOTTE - Because sometimes one may happen to be so low in Spirits, as not to know one's own Mind; and then, you know, if a foolish Husband should happen to say a Word on either Side, why one determines on the contrary without any farther Trouble.

CAPT BELLAMANT - Right, Madam, and a thousand to one, but the happy Rogue, your Husband, might warm his indolent Inclinations too from the same Spirit of Contradiction, ha, ha.

LADY CHARLOTTE - Well, I am so passionately fond of my own Humour, That let me die, if a Husband were to insist upon my never missing any one Diversion this Town affords, I believe in my Conscience, I should go twice a Day to Church, to avoid 'em.

CAPT BELLAMANT - O fy! you could not be so unfashionable a Creature!

LADY CHARLOTTE - Ay, but I would tho'. I do not care what I do, when I'm vext.

CAPT BELLAMANT - Well! let me perish, this is a most delectable Scheme. Don't you think, Madam, we shall be vastly happy?

LADY CHARLOTTE - We, what we? pray, who do you mean, Sir?

CAPT BELLAMANT - Why, Lady Betty Shuttlecock and I: Why you must know this is the very Scheme she laid down to me last Night; which so vastly charm'd me, that we resolv'd to be married upon it to–morrow Morning.

LADY CHARLOTTE - What do you mean?

CAPT BELLAMANT - Only to take your Advice, Madam, by allowing my Wife all the modish Privileges, that you seem so passionately fond of.

LADY CHARLOTTE - Your Wife? why, who's to be your Wife, pray? you don't think of me, I hope.

CAPT BELLAMANT - One wou'd think, you thought I did: for you refuse me as odly, as if I had ask'd you the Question: Not, but I suppose, you would have me think now, you have refus'd me in earnest.

LADY CHARLOTTE - Ha! ha! ha! that's well enough; why, sweet Sir, do you really think I am not in Earnest?

CAPT BELLAMANT - No faith, I can't think you're so silly, as to refuse me in Earnest, when I only ask'd you in Jest. [Both.] Ha! ha! ha!

LADY CHARLOTTE - Ridiculous!

CAPT BELLAMANT - Delightful! well, after all, I am a strange Creature to be so merry, when I am just going to be married.

LADY CHARLOTTE - And had you ever the Assurance to think I would have you?

CAPT BELLAMANT - Why, faith! I don't know, but I might, if I had ever made love to youWell, Lady Charlotte, your Servant. I suppose you'll come and visit my Wife, as soon as ever she sees Company.

LADY CHARLOTTE - What do you mean?

CAPT BELLAMANT - Seriously what I say, Madam; I am just now going to my Lawyer to sign my Marriage Articles with Lady Betty Shuttlecock.

LADY CHARLOTTE - And are you going in Earnest?

CAPT BELLAMANT - Positively. Seriously.

LADY CHARLOTTE - Then I must take the Liberty to tell you, Sir, you are the greatest Villain, that ever liv'd upon the Face of the Earth.

CAPT BELLAMANT - Ha! what do I see? [She burst into Tears.] Is it possible! O my dear! dear Lady Charlotte, can I believe my self the Cause of these transporting Tears! O! till this Instant never did I taste of Happiness.

LADY CHARLOTTE - Ha! ha! nor I upon my Faith, Sir! Ha! ha!

CAPT BELLAMANT - Hey day! what do you mean?

LADY CHARLOTTE - That you are one of the silliest Animals, that ever open'd his Lips to a WomanHa! ha! O I shall die! ha! ha!

Enter a Servant.

SERVANT - Sir, here's a Letter for you.

CAPT BELLAMANT - So, it's come in good time. If this does not give her a turn, Egad, I shall have all my Plague to go over again. Lady Charlotte , you'll give me leave.

LADY CHARLOTTE - O Sir! Billet doux are exempt from Ceremony. Ha! ha!

CAPT BELLAMANT - [After reading to himself.] Ha! ha! Well, my dear Lady Charlotte, I am vastly glad to see you are so easy; upon my Soul, I was afraid you was really in love with me; But since I need have no farther Apprehensions of it, I know you won't take it ill, if I obey the Summons of my Wife, that is to beLady Betty has sent for meYou'll excuse me if I am confin'd a Week or two, with my Wife for the present; When that's over, you and I will laugh and sing, and coquette as much as ever we did, and so dear Lady Charlotte, your humble Servant.

[Exit.

LADY CHARLOTTE - What can the Creature mean? I know not what to think of him! sure it can't be true! but if it should be true. I can't believe it true and yet it may be true too. I am resolv'd to be satisfiedHere, who's there! will no Body hear? Who's there, I say.

Enter Servant.

Desire Captain Bellamant to step back again.

SERVANT - He's just gone out, Madam.

LADY CHARLOTTE - Then it's certainly trueget me a Chair this Momentthis Instantgo, run, fly! I am in such a Hurry, I don't know what I do. O hideous! I look horridly frightfulbut I'll follow him just as I amI'll go to Lady Betty'sIf I find him there, I shall certainly faint. I must take a little Hartshorn with me.

[Exit.

SCENE X

Mr. Gaywit, Mrs. Modern, meeting in his Lodgings.

MR GAYWIT - This is exactly the Time I appointed her to meet me here. Ha! she comes, you are punctual as a young Lover to his first Appointment.

MRS MODERN - Women commonly begin to be most punctual, when Men leave it off; our Passions seldom reach their Meridian,
before yours set.

MR GAYWIT - We can no more help the Decrease of our Passions, than you the Increase of yours; and tho' like the Sun I was obliged to quit your Hemisphere, I have left you a Moon to shine in it.

MRS MODERN - What do you mean?

MR GAYWIT - I suppose you are by this no Stranger to the Fondness of the Gentleman I introduced to you; nor will you shortly be to his Generosity. He is one who has more Money than Brains, and more Generosity than Money.

MRS MODERN - Oh! Gaywit! I am undone: you will too soon know how; will hear it perhaps with Pleasure, since it is too plain by betraying me to your Friend; I have no longer any Share in your Love.

MR GAYWIT - Blame not my Inconstancy, but your own.

MRS MODERN - By all our Joys I never loved another.

MR GAYWIT - Nay, will you deny what Conviction has long since constrained you to own? Will you deny your Favours to Lord Richly?

MRS MODERN - He had indeed my Person, but you alone my Heart.

MR GAYWIT - I always take a Woman's Person to be the strongest Assurance of her Heart. I think, the Love of a Mistress who gives up her Person, is no more to be doubted than the Love of a Friend who gives you his Purse.

MRS MODERN - By Heavens, I hate and despise him equal with my Husband. And as I was forced to marry the latter by the Commands of my Parents, so I was given up to the former by the Intreaties of my Husband.

MR GAYWIT - By the Intreaties of your Husband!

MRS MODERN - Hell and his blacker Soul both know the Truth of what I sayThat he betrayed me first, and has ever since been the Pander of our Amour; to you my own Inclinations led me. Lord Richly has paid for his Pleasures, to you they have still been free: He was my Husband's Choice, but you alone were mine.

MR GAYWIT - And have you not complied with Bellamant too?

MRS MODERN - Oh! blame not my Necessities. He is indeed that generous Creature you have spoke him.

MR GAYWIT - And have you not betrayed this generous Creature to a Wretch?

MRS MODERN - I see you know it allBy Heavens I have not: It was his own Jealousy, not my Design; nay, he importuned me to have discovered Lord Richly in the same manner; Oh, think not any Hopes could have prevailed on me to blast my Fame. No Reward could make me amends for that Loss. Thou shalt see by my Retirement I have a Soul too great to encounter Shame.

MR GAYWIT - I will try to make that Retirement easy to you; and call me not ungrateful for attempting to discomfit your Husband's Purpose, and preserve my Friend.

MRS MODERN - I my self will preserve him; if my Husband pursues his Intentions, my Woman will swear that the Servant own'd he was hired to be a false Evidence against us.

MR GAYWIT - Then since the Story is already publick, forgive this last Blush I am obliged to put you to.

MRS MODERN - What do you mean?

MR GAYWIT - These Witnesses must inform you.

SCENE XI

Mr. Gaywit, Mr. Bellamant, Mrs. Bellamant, Mrs. Modern, Emilia, Capt. Merit.

MRS MODERN - Distraction! Tortures!

MR GAYWIT - I have with Difficulty brought myself to give you this Shock; which nothing but the Preservation of the best of Friends could have extorted; and which you shall be made amends for.

MR BELLAMANT - Be not shocked, Madam; it shall be your Husband's Fault, if you are farther uneasy on this Account.

MR GAYWIT - Come, Madam, you may your self reap a Benefit from what I have done, since it may prevent your being exposed in another Place.

MRS MODERN - All Places to me are equal, except this.

[Exit.

MRS BELLAMANT - Her Misfortunes move my Compassion.

MR GAYWIT - It is generous in you, Madam, to pity the Misfortunes of a Woman, whose Faults are more her Husband's than her
own.

SCENE XII

Lord Richly, Mr. Modern, Mr. Gaywit, Mr. Bellamant, Mrs. Bellamant, Emilia

LORD RICHLY - Mr. Gaywit, upon my Word, you have the most splendid Levée I have seen.

MR GAYWIT - I am sorry, my Lord, you have increased it by one who should only grace the Keeper of Newgate's Levée; a Fellow whose Company is scandalous to your Lordship, as it is odious to us all.

MR BELLAMANT - His Lordship is not the only Man who goes abroad with his Cuckold.

LORD RICHLY - Methinks you have invited a Gentleman to a very scurvy Entertainment.

MR GAYWIT - You'll know, my Lord very shortly, wherefore he was invited, and how much you your self are obliged to his kind endeavours; for would his Wife have consented to his Intreaties, this pretended Discovery had fallen on you, and you had supplied that Gentleman's Place.

LORD RICHLY - A Discovery fallen on me!

CAPT MERIT - Yes, my Lord, the whole Company are Witnesses to Mrs. Modern's Confession of it; that he betrayed her to your Embraces with a Design to discover you in them.

MR MODERN - My Lord, this is a base Design to ruin the humblest of your Creatures in your Lordship's Favour.

LORD RICHLY - How it should have that Effect I know not; for I do not understand a Word of what these Gentlemen mean.

MR GAYWIT - We shall convince your Lordship; in the mean time I must beg you to leave this Apartment; you may prosecute what Revenge you please, but at Law we shall dare to defy you. The Damages will not be very great, which are given to a voluntary Cuckold.

EMILIA - Tho' I see not why; for it is surely as much a Robbery to take away a Picture unpaid for, from the Painter who would sell it, as from the Gentleman who would keep it.

MR MODERN - You may have your Jest, Madam, but I will be paid severely for it; I shall have a Time of laughing in my Turn. My Lord, your most obedient Servant.

SCENE XIII

Lord Richly, Mr. Gaywit, Mr. Bellamant, Captain Bellamant, Lady Charlotte, Mrs. Bellamant, Emilia

MR GAYWIT - He will find his Mistake, and our Conquest soon enough; and now, my Lord, I hope you will ratify that Consent you gave me this Morning, and compleat my Happiness with this Lady.

LORD RICHLY - Truly, Nephew, you misunderstood me, if you imagined I promised any such thing: However, tho' you know I might insist on my Brother's Will; yet let Mr. Bellamant give his Daughter a Fortune equal to yours, and I shall not oppose it; and till then I shall not consent.

MR GAYWIT - Hah!

CAPT BELLAMANT - I hope your Lordship has not determined to deny every Request; and therefore I may hope your Blessing.

[Kneels.

LORD RICHLY - What does this mean?

CAPT BELLAMANT - Lady Charlotte, my Lord, has given me this Right. Your Daughter

LORD RICHLY - What of her?

CAPT BELLAMANT - Is my Wife.

LORD RICHLY - Your Wife!

CAPT BELLAMANT - Nay, if you will not give me your Blessing, you may let it alone: I would not kneel any longer to you, tho' you were the great Mogul.

LORD RICHLY - Very well! this is your doing, Mr. Bellamant, or rather my own. Confusion! my Estate, my Title, and my Daughter, all contribute to aggrandize the Man I must hate, because he knows I would have wronged him! Well, Sirs! whatever Pleasures you may seem to take at my several Disappointments, I shall take very little Trouble to be revenged on any of you; being heartily convinced, that in a few Months you will be so many mutual Plagues to one another.

SCENE the last.

Mr. Gaywit, Mr. Bellamant, Captain Bellamant, Lady Charlotte, Mrs. Bellamant, Emilia

MR BELLAMANT - Methinks, I might have been consulted on this Affair.

LADY CHARLOTTE - We had no time for Consultation; our Amour has been of a very short Date.

CAPT BELLAMANT - All our Love is to come, Lady Charlotte.

LADY CHARLOTTE - I expect a deal of Love after Marriage, for what I have bated you before it.

CAPT BELLAMANT - I never asked you the Question till I was sure of you.

LADY CHARLOTTE - Then you knew my Mind better than myself; for I never resolved to have you, till I had you.

MR GAYWIT - Now, my dear Emilia, there is no Bar in our way to Happiness. Lady Charlotte has made my Lord's Consent unnecessary too: Your Father has already blessed me with his, and it is now in your Power to make me the happiest of Mankind.

EMILIA - I suppose, you follow my Brother's Method, and never ask till you are sure of obtaining.

MR BELLAMANT - Gaywit, my Obligations to you are beyond my Power of repaying; and while I give you what you ask, I am still heaping greater Favours on my self.

MR GAYWIT - Think not so, when you bestow on me more than any Man can merit.

MR BELLAMANT - Then take the little all I have, and may you be as happy with her, as I am in these Arms; [Embracing Mrs. Bellamant.] whence the whole World should never estrange me more.

MRS BELLAMANT - I am too happy in that Resolution.

MR GAYWIT - Lady Charlotte! I made a Promise this Day to your Father in your Favour; which I am resolved to keep, tho' he hath broken his. I know, your good Nature and good Sense will forgive a Fault which Love has made me commitLove, which directs our Inclinations in spight of equal and superior Charms.

LADY CHARLOTTE - No Excuses, dear Sir, my Inclinations were as whimsical as yours.

CAPT BELLAMANT - You have fairly got the Start, Lady Charlotte.

MR GAYWIT - My Bellamant! my Friend! my Father! What a Transport do I feel from the Prospect of adding to your future Happiness! Let us henceforth be one Family, and have no other Contest but to outvy in Love.

MR BELLAMANT - My Son! Oh! What Happiness do I owe to thy Friendship, and may the Example of my late Misfortune warn thee to fly all such Encounters; and since we are setting out together in the Road to Happiness, take this Truth from an experienced Traveller. However slight the Consequence may prove, Which waits unmarried Libertines in Love, Be from all Vice divorc'd before you wed, And bury Falshood in the bridal Bed.

EPILOGUE

Spoken by Mrs. HERON

In dull Retirement e're I go to Grieve,
Ladies, I am return'd, to take my Leave:
Prudes, I suppose, will, with their old good Nature,
Shew their great Vertue, and condemn the Creature:
They fail not at th' Unfortunate to Flout,
Not because Naughtybut becausefound out.
Why, faithif these Discoveries succeed,

Marriage will soon become a Trade, indeed!
This Trade, I'm sure, will flourish in the Nation,
'Twill be esteem'd below no Man of Fashion,
To be a Member of the Cuckold's Corporation!
What Int'rest will be made! what mighty doing!
To be Directors for the Year ensuing!
And 'tis exceeding difficult to say,
Which end of this chaste Town wou'd win the Day:
Oh! shou'd no Chance this Corporation stop,
Where shou'd we find one House, without a Shop?
How wou'd a Wife hung out, draw Beaux in Throngs!
To hire your Dears, like Domino's, at Long's!
There wou'd be dainty Days! when every Ninny,
Might put them on and offfor half a Guinea!
Oh! to behold th' embroider'd Trader grin,
My Wife's at HomePray, Gentlemen, walk in!
Money alone Men will no more importune,
When ev'ry Beauty makes her Husband's Fortune!
While Juries value Vertue at this Rate,
Each Wife is (when discover'd) an Estate!
A Wife with Gold, is mixing Gall with Honey,
But here you lose your Wife by what you get your Money.
And now, t'obey a dull Poetic Sentence,
In lonely Woods, I must pursue Repentance!
Ye Virgins pure, ye modest Matrons, lend
Attentive Ears to your departing Friend;
If Fame, unspotted, be the Thing you drive at,
Be Vertuous, if you can, if not, be Private
But hold! Why shou'd I leave my Sister–Sinners,
To dwell 'mongst Innocents, or young Beginners?
Frailty will better with the Frail go down;
So hang the Stupid Bard! I'll stay in Town.

Henry Fielding – A Short Biography

Henry Fielding was born at Sharpham Park, near Glastonbury, in Somerset on April 22nd 1707. His early years were spent on his parents' farm in Dorset. His family were well to do. His father was a colonel, later a general in the army, his maternal grandfather was a judge of the Queen's Bench and his second cousin would later become the fourth Earl of Denbigh.

He was educated at Eton where he became lifelong friends with William Pitt the Elder.

An early romance ended disastrously and with it his removal to London and the beginnings of a glittering literary career. Early advice on this came from another cousin, the noted poet, Lady Mary Wortley Montagu. Fielding published his first play, at age 21, in 1728.

Later that same year he journeyed to the University at Leiden, the oldest University in Holland, to study classics and law. However, within months, with funds low, mainly due to his father cutting off his allowance, he was forced to return to London and to write for the theatre.

It was a twist of fate that was to ensure him both notoriety and a reputation that would exceed his wildest expectations.

He was prolific, sometimes writing six plays a year, but he did like to poke fun at the authorities. His plays were thought to be the final straw for the authorities in their attempts to bring some sense of order to an increasingly provocative Theatre. Some of the plays denigrated, insulted, or criticised either the King, or his Government, in ways that caused them to react with their preferred response; a new law. Although the Golden Rump was cited as the play on which the authorities based their need for better regulation it is thought that the constant stepping over the line by Fielding in his own works was the actual trigger for, and target of, the new law. No copy of the play, The Golden Rump, exists today and it seems never, in fact, to have been performed or perhaps even published. Various accounts attribute Fielding as the author and others say it was secretly commissioned by Walpole himself to bring about the conditions necessary to bring the Act before Parliament.

Whatever the validity in 1737 The Theatrical Licensing Act was passed. At a stroke political satire was almost impossible. Fielding much admired – and reviled – for his savaging of Sir Robert Walpole government was rendered mute. Any playwright who was viewed with suspicion by the Government now found an audience difficult to find and therefore Theatre owners now toed the Government line, works only being available for performance after review by the Lord Chamberlain. A process that was to last in England, although greatly amended in 1843, until 1968.

Fielding was practical in the circumstances and ironically stopped writing to once again take up his career in the practice of law. He became a barrister after studying at Middle Temple – he completed the six year course in only three. By this time he had also married Charlotte Craddock, his first wife, and they would go on to have five children, but only a daughter would survive. Charlotte died in 1744 but was immortalised as the heroine in both Tom Jones and Amelia.

As a businessman Fielding lacked any financial education and he and his family often endured bouts of poverty. He did however find a wealthy benefactor in the shape of Ralph Allen, who was to later feature in the novel Tom Jones as the character foundation for Squire Allworthy.

Fielding never stopped writing political satire or satires of current arts and letters. The Tragedy of Tragedies, for which Hogarth designed the frontispiece, had, for example, some success as a printed play. He also contributed a number of works to journals of the day as well as writing for Tory periodicals, usually under the name of "Captain Hercules Vinegar". His choice of name reveals his style. But then again his other later nom de plumes are also revealing; Sir Alexander Drawcansir and Scriblerus Secundus

In 1731 Fielding wrote "The Roast Beef of Old England", which is used by the Royal Navy and the United States Marine Corps. It was later arranged by Richard Leveridge.

During the late 1730s and early 1740s Fielding continued to air his liberal and anti-Jacobite views in satirical articles and newspapers. He was nothing if not passionate and this adherence to principles would eventually have great reward for him.

Fielding was much put out by the success of Samuel Richardson's Pamela, or Virtue Rewarded. His reaction was to spur him into writing a novel. In 1741 this first novel, Shamela, was a success, an anonymous parody of Richardson's melodramatic novel. It is a satire that follows the model of the famous Tory satirists of the previous generation; Swift and Gay.

On the tail of this success came Joseph Andrews in 1742. Begun as a parody on Pamela's brother, Joseph, it swiftly developed and matured into an accomplished novel in its own right and marked the entrance of Fielding as a major English novelist.

In 1743, he published a novel in the Miscellanies volume III (which was, in fact, the first volume of the Miscellanies). This was The History of the Life of the Late Mr Jonathan Wild the Great. Sometimes this is cited as his first novel, as he did indeed begin writing it before Shamela, but it is now placed later. Once again Fielding returns to satire and one of his favourite subjects – Sir Robert Walpole. In it he draws a parallel between Walpole and Jonathan Wild, the infamous gang leader and highwayman. He implicitly compares the Whig party in Parliament to a gang of thieves, whose leader, Walpole, lives only for his desire and ambition to be a "Great Man" (a common epithet for Walpole) and should culminate only in the antithesis of greatness: being hung from a gallows. By now Walpole had resigned as Prime minster after some 20 years. Fielding could now re-affirm political allegiance back to the Whigs and would now denounce both Tories and Jacobites in his writings.

Although Fielding was never afraid to court controversy he published his next work anonymously in 1746, and perhaps with good reason. The Female Husband, a fictionalized account of a sensational case of a female transvestite who was tried for duping another woman into marriage. This was one of a number of small published pamphlets at sixpence a time. Though a minor item in both length and his canon it shows Fielding's consistent interest and examination of fraud, sham, and masks but, of course, his subject matter was rather sensational.

In 1747, three years after Charlotte's death and ignoring public opinion, he married her former maid, Mary Daniel, who was pregnant. Mary bore him five children altogether; three daughters, who died early and sons William and Allen.

Undoubtedly the masterpiece of Fielding's career was the novel Tom Jones, published in 1749. It is a wonderfully and carefully constructed picaresque novel following the convoluted and hilarious tale of how a foundling came into a fortune.

Fielding was a consistent anti-Jacobite and a keen supporter of the Church of England. This led to him now being richly rewarded with the position of London's Chief Magistrate. The position itself had no salary attached but he refused all manner of bribes during his tenure, which was most unusual. Fielding continued to write and his career both literary and professional continued to climb.

In 1749 he joined with his younger half-brother John, to help found what was the nascent forerunner to a London police force, the Bow Street Runners. (He and his siblings were quite some partnership. His younger sister, Sarah, also became a well known novelist)

His influence here was undoubted. He and John did much to help the cause of judicial reform and to help improve prison conditions. His pamphlets and enquiries included a proposal for the abolition of public hangings. This was not, as you would think because he was opposed to capital punishment as such—indeed, for example, in his 1751 presiding over the trial of the notorious criminal James Field, he found him guilty in a robbery and sentenced him to hang.

In January 1752 Fielding started a fortnightly periodical titled The Covent-Garden Journal, which he would publish under the colourful pseudonym of "Sir Alexander Drawcansir, Knt. Censor of Great Britain" until November of the same year. In this periodical, Fielding directly challenged the "armies of Grub Street" and the other periodical writers of the day in a conflict that would eventually become the Paper War of 1752–3.

Fielding then published, in 1753, "Examples of the interposition of Providence in the Detection and Punishment of Murder, a work in which, rejecting the deistic and materialistic visions of the world, he wrote in favour of the belief in God's presence and divine judgement, arguing that the rise of murder rates was due to neglect of the Christian religion. In 1753 he would add to this with Proposals for making an effectual Provision for the Poor.

Fielding's ardent commitment to the cause of justice as a great humanitarian in the 1750s unfortunately coincided with a rapid deterioration in his health. Such was his decline that in the summer of 1754 he travelled, with Mary and his daughter, to Portugal in search of a cure. Gout, asthma, dropsy and other afflictions forced him to use crutches. His health continued to fail alarmingly.

Henry Fielding died in Lisbon two months later on October 8th, 1754.

His tomb is in the city's English Cemetery (Cemitério Inglês), which is now the graveyard of St. George's Church, Lisbon.

Henry Fielding – A Concise Bibliography

The Masquerade, a poem
Love in Several Masques, a play, 1728
Rape Upon Rape, a play, 1730.
The Temple Beau, a play, 1730
The Author's Farce, a play, 1730
The Letter Writers, a play, 1731
The Tragedy of Tragedies; or, The Life and Death of Tom Thumb the Great, a play, 1731
Grub-Street Opera, a play, 1731
The Roast Beef of Old England, 1731
The Modern Husband, a play, 1732
The Mock Doctor, a play, 1732
The Lottery, a play, 1732
The Covent Garden Tragedy, a play, 1732
The Miser, a play, 1732
The Old Debauchees, a play 1732
The Intriguing Chambermaid, a play, 1734
Don Quixote in England, a play, 1734
Pasquin, a play, 1736
Eurydice Hiss'd, a play, 1737
The Historical Register for the Year 1736, a play, 1737
An Apology for the Life of Mrs. Shamela Andrews, a novel, 1741
The History of the Adventures of Joseph Andrews & his Friend, Mr. Abraham Abrams, a novel, 1742
The Life and Death of Jonathan Wild, the Great, a novel, 1743.
Miscellanies – collection of works, 1743, contained the poem Part of Juvenal's Sixth Satire, Modernized in Burlesque Verse
The Female Husband or the Surprising History of Mrs Mary alias Mr George Hamilton, who was convicted of having married a young woman of Wells and lived with her as her husband, taken from her own mouth since her confinement, a pamphlet, fictionalized report, 1746
The History of Tom Jones, a Foundling, a novel, 1749

A Journey from this World to the Next – 1749

Amelia, a novel, 1751

"Examples of the interposition of Providence in the Detection and Punishment of Murder containing above thirty cases in which this dreadful crime has been brought to light in the most extraordinary and miraculous manner; collected from various authors, ancient and modern", 1752

The Covent Garden Journal, a periodical, 1752

Journal of a Voyage to Lisbon, a travel narrative, 1755

The Fathers: Or, the Good-Natur'd Man, a play, published posthumously in 1778

Other Works (Undated)

An Old Man or The Virgin Unmasked

Miss Lucy in Town, a Play, a sequel to The Virgin Unmasked

Plutus with William Young from the Greek play by Aristophanes.

The Temple Beau, a play

The Wedding Beau, a play

The Welsh Opera

Tumble-Down Dick

An Essay on Conversation, an Essay

The True Patriot, a letter